# Genetics and Experience

# Sage Series on Individual Differences and Development

Robert Plomin, *Series Editor*

The purpose of the Sage Series on Individual Differences and Development is to provide a forum for a new wave of research that focuses on individual differences in behavioral development. A powerful theory of development must be able to explain individual differences, rather than just average developmental trends, if for no other reason than that large differences among individuals exist for all aspects of development. Variance—the very standard deviation—represents a major part of the phenomenon to be explained. There are three other reasons for studying individual differences in development: First, developmental issues of greatest relevance to society are issues of individual differences. Second, descriptions and explanations of normative aspects of development bear no necessary relationship to those of individual differences in development. Third, questions concerning the processes underlying individual differences in development are more easily answered than questions concerning the origins of normative aspects of development.

## Editorial Board

## Books in This Series

# Genetics and Experience

## The Interplay Between Nature and Nurture

## Robert Plomin

Individual
Differences
and
Development
Series
**VOLUME 6**

**SAGE** Publications
*International Educational and Professional Publisher*
Thousand Oaks   London   New Delhi

*For information address:*

SAGE Publications, Inc.
2455 Teller Road
Thousand Oaks, California 91320

SAGE Publications Ltd.
6 Bonhill Street
London EC2A 4PU
United Kingdom

SAGE Publications India Pvt. Ltd.
M-32 Market
Greater Kailash I
New Delhi 110 048 India


Printed in the United States of America

**Library of Congress Cataloging-in-Publication Data**

Plomin, Robert, 1948-
  Genetics and experience: the interplay between nature and nuture
/Robert Plomin.
    p. cm.—(Sage series on individual differences and
development : vol. 6)
  Includes bibliographical references.
  ISBN 0-8039-5420-4.—ISBN 0-8039-5421-2 (pbk.)
  1. Nature and nurture. 2. Individual differences. 3. Genetic
psychology. I. Title. II. Series.
BF341.P55   1994
155.7—dc20                                                        93-41841
                                                                       CIP



94  95  96  97  10  9  8  7  6  5  4  3  2  1

Sage Production Editor: Judith L. Hunter

# Contents

# Tables and Figures

*To the memory of Steven G. Vandenberg*

# Preface

This book explores the hyphen in the phrase *nature-nurture*. The hyphen is somewhat like the rabbit hole in *Alice in Wonderland*. After tumbling down the hole, a quick glance around at this new world shows it to be an expanding universe with galaxies of related issues. Because this book must be brief, exploration of this hyphen-turned-universe requires a telescopic focus on a few features of the terrain. The focus of this book is nurture (environment) as viewed from the perspective of nature (genetics).

The book's purview is limited in ways implied by the phrase *nature-nurture*. Most importantly, the book is limited to individual differences. It considers nurture and nature in terms of their interplay in the development of characteristics that differ among members of the human species rather than characteristics that are typically manifested by members of our species. In relation to genetics, it considers DNA differences among individuals that are heritable in the Mendelian sense of transmission from generation to generation rather than the vast majority of DNA that is the same for all members of our species. Similarly, the focus is on environmental differences such as differences in the language-learning environment that parents provide for their children, rather than the fact that nearly all members of our species are exposed to language early in life. This focus on the etiology of variations on species-typical themes helps to keep the discussion empirically grounded because the etiology of individual differences is more amenable to empirical investigation than species-typical development (Plomin, DeFries, & Fulker, 1988).

Although it is important to consider species-wide themes as well as variations on these themes (Mayr, 1982; McCall, 1981; Scarr, 1992), it is also important to emphasize the distinction between them because the processes involved in the development of individual differences can differ greatly from the processes responsible for species-typical development. For example, our species has evolved to use language naturally, requiring only minimal exposure to the species' evolutionarily expected environment. However, it is likely that differences among children in their facility with language are at least in part due to differences in the language-learning environments provided by their parents. This issue and basic theory and methods of quantitative genetics as they are applied to the study of individual differences in behavior are described elsewhere (Plomin, 1990a; Plomin, DeFries, & McClearn, 1990).

Not only is the book limited to viewing nurture from the perspective of nature, it also focuses on just one feature of this view. The core of the book is an important empirical phenomenon that has been discovered during the past decade: Genetic factors contribute to measures of the environment that are widely used in the behavioral sciences. This phenomenon, which could be called the nature of nurture, is useful in providing an empirical grounding for a discussion of what is meant by nature, by nurture, and by the interplay between them.

The book begins with a general discussion of what we mean by nature and what we mean by nurture, with an eye on the hyphen between them. It attempts to show that contemporary research and theory in genetics and in environment are evolving toward each other. Without a doubt, some of the most interesting questions for genetic research involve the environment and some of the most interesting questions for environmental research involve genetics.

Chapters 2 and 3 document the phenomenon of the genetic contribution to environmental measures for familial and extrafamilial environments, respectively. The hyphen itself comes back to center stage in the final two chapters. Chapter 4 asks what mediates this genetic contribution to environmental measures. Chapter 5 presents a theory of the genetics of experience. The argument developed is that finding genetic influence on environmental measures does not simply imply that environmental measures ought to be cleaned up so that they are no longer influenced by genetic factors. The larger issue is that genetic factors contribute to experience itself. That is, genetics plays a role in the active selection, modification, and even creation of environments. This provides a window through which the hyphen between nature-nurture can be explored empirically.

I am grateful to C. Deborah Laughton, the Sage Editor of this series, for suggesting that I write this book, and to Judy Dunn for her wise counsel throughout the book's development. The book has profited considerably from reviews by Dorothy Bishop, Avshalom Caspi, Craig Edelbrock, John Loehlin, Michael Rutter, Jim Stevenson, Irwin Waldman, and Ted Wachs. The book was written on sabbatical leave from The Pennsylvania State University, supported by a James McKeen Cattell Sabbatical Award, a Fogarty Senior International Fellowship, and a Fulbright Scholar Award. Research on genetics and experience was gleaned from several longitudinal behavioral genetic projects generously supported for many years. The Colorado Adoption Project (J. C. DeFries, D. W. Fulker, and R. Plomin, coinvestigators) is supported by the National Institute of Child Health and Human Development (HD-10333, HD-18426) and the National Institute of Mental Health (MH-43899). An extension of the Colorado Adoption Project on mother-sibling interactions (J. Dunn, D. W. Fulker, and R. Plomin) is supported by the National Science Foundation (BNS-9108749). Support for the Nonshared Environment in Adolescent Development project (E. M. Hetherington, R. Plomin, and D. Reiss) is provided by the National Institute of Mental Health (MH-43383). The Swedish Adoption/Twin Study of Aging (G. E. McClearn, N. Pedersen, and R. Plomin) is supported by the National Institute of Aging (AG-04563) and the MacArthur Foundation Research Network on Successful Aging. I am also grateful to my current and recent predoctoral and postdoctoral students who have done most of the work: Cindy Bergeman, Julia Braungart, Heather Chipuer, Beth Manke, Shirley McGuire, Jenaè Neiderhiser, Alison Pike, Richard Rende, and Kim Saudino. David Rowe, the first graduate student with whom I worked, conducted the pioneering research in this field more than a decade ago.

Finally, I dedicate this book to the father of the modern era of human behavioral genetics, Steven G. Vandenberg, who died August 27, 1992. His papers on twin research in the 1960s were among the first papers I ever read in behavioral genetics. The creativity and clarity of these papers drew me into the field. As a graduate student, I never dreamed that I would be lucky enough to be his colleague at the Institute for Behavioral Genetics in Boulder, Colorado. He was a walking library—I have yet to meet anyone who knows as much about so many things. Always eager to talk, he was full of good ideas that he shared freely, even with a new assistant professor.

# 1

# Nature and Nurture

The geneticist C. D. Darlington, in a popular 1953 book called *The Facts of Life*, foreshadowed the main themes of this book, almost offhandedly. He suggested that genetics contributes to experience, and he succinctly described the processes of passive, reactive, and active genotype-environment correlation, which are central to the present book:

> In this world no two individuals have to put up with the same environment: we have a choice. . . . It may be a passive choice in which we accept one of the possibilities that is offered to us. Heredity may then indeed be said to "respond" to the environment as the textbooks tell us. But it may be an active selection. We may even create to a greater or lesser extent the environment we want. (Darlington, 1953, p. 302)

Darlington's book received a scathing review by two other well-known geneticists, Th. Dobzhansky and L. S. Penrose. Their criticisms centered on the book's hereditarian bias, but they specifically took exception to Darlington's suggestion that genetics contributes to experience:

> Most readers will have plenty of evidence ready to hand indicating that environments in which men live are tremendously diversified

1

and that this diversity influences human personality. To counteract this bias, the author offers a theory of his own, which can be admired as a *tour de force* of casuistry. It is as follows: man chooses his environment; the environment chosen is determined by the genotype of one who chooses; *ergo*, the environmental effects are not environmental but genetic! (Dobzhansky & Penrose, 1955, p. 77)

With proper qualification, this "tour de force of casuistry" is the theme of the present book. The qualifications are important: People *to some extent* choose their environments; the environments chosen are *influenced by*, not "determined by," the genotypes of those who choose. Moreover, many environments are not chosen as much as imposed, but these, too, could be imposed to some extent on the basis of genetically influenced characteristics of individuals. The real difference, however, is data. The goal of this book is to review recent research that has investigated this issue. Darlington's hypothesis of a correlation between genetics and experience is no longer guilty of the charge of casuistry because research consistently converges on the conclusion that genetic factors contribute to many widely used measures of the environment. Chapters 2 and 3 review relevant research. Chapter 4 explores factors responsible for the genetic contributions to measures of the environment and Chapter 5 presents a theory of genetics and experience.

The purpose of this chapter is to examine what is currently meant by nature and by nurture, with the goal of showing that modern theory and research on both nature and nurture are converging on the interface between them. Some of the most interesting and fundamental questions about genetics, even at the level of the molecular biology of DNA, involve the environment. Similarly, some of the most interesting and fundamental questions about the environment involve genetics. Unlike subsequent chapters, which are relentlessly empirical, this chapter provides a general discussion of current issues in the fields of molecular biology and of environmental research. Readers who are impatient to get to the data are encouraged to skip to the next chapter.

The relationship between nature and nurture has been discussed since antiquity. The modern discussion began with a cousin of

Charles Darwin, Francis Galton. Galton coined the phrase *nature-nurture* in the scientific arena. For Galton, the question was the relative importance of nature and nurture. He left no doubt as to which he considered to be most important:

> There is no escape from the conclusion that nature prevails enormously over nurture when the differences of nurture do not exceed what is commonly to be found among persons of the same rank in the same country. (Galton, 1883, p. 241)

During the first few decades of this century, similarly extreme hereditarian views were held by other scientists. These views collided with the emerging environmentalist extremism best portrayed by Watson, who argued that "there is no such thing as an inheritance of capacity, talent, temperament, mental constitution and characteristics" (Watson, 1925, p. 74). In what must be the most quoted quote in psychology, Watson's give-me-a-dozen-healthy-infants challenge in his book *Behaviorism* was reiterated throughout his writings:

> The behaviorists believe that there is nothing from within to develop. If you start with the right number of fingers and toes, eyes, and a few elementary movements that are present at birth, you do not need anything else in the way of raw material to make a man, be that man genius, a cultured gentleman, a rowdy or a thug. (Watson, 1928, p. 41)

Is there a single scientist today who truly believes in either the hereditarian or environmentalist extreme? A century of research in the field of behavioral genetics has shown that genetic influence is significant and substantial for most areas of behavioral development, even though it is not true that "nature prevails enormously over nurture" (Plomin & McClearn, 1993). For some traits such as cognitive abilities, genetic differences among individuals can account for about half of the variance in test scores. Seldom in the behavioral sciences do we find factors that account for so much variance. Most of the statistically significant findings that fill our textbooks account for less than 5% of the variance. Nonetheless, if genetic differences account for half of the variance, this means that genetic differences do not account for the other half. As an antidote to the mistaken notion that the goal of behavioral genetics is to demonstrate that everything is genetic, I would argue that behavioral genetic research has provided the best available evidence for the importance of the environment.

It was a reasonable first step in nature-nurture research to ask how much nature and nurture contribute to variability in behavioral development. If heredity were unimportant, as most psychologists believed during the reign of environmentalism in the 1950s and 1960s, it is irrelevant to ask how nature and nurture interact during development. Similarly, if environment is viewed as unimportant, it is not interesting to ask how nature and nurture interact during development. Such a view is probably inconceivable for most behavioral scientists. However, as the research pendulum swings from nurture to nature in many fields such as psychiatry, it is important to emphasize the point just made: The same quantitative genetic data that have made the case for the importance of genetic differences also provide strong evidence for the importance of nongenetic factors. Moreover, quantitative genetic methods facilitate new approaches to understanding the environment—one of these approaches is the theme of this book.

The main reason why nature-nurture research has focused on the "how much" question rather than the "how" question (Anastasi, 1958) is that the methods of human quantitative genetics, twin and adoption studies, have been available to address the "how much" question. The "how" question is more difficult. At the outset, it should be emphasized that this book makes no pretense of addressing the "how" question in its general form. This is a multifaceted question and very few of its facets seem susceptible to empirical investigation. Instead, the keystone for this book is a finding that has emerged during the past decade: Many measures widely used in the behavioral sciences as indices of the environment show a genetic contribution. Chapters 2 and 3 describe this phenomenon, and the rest of the book attempts to interpret it.

The first half of this chapter sets the stage by discussing new developments in genetic theory and research in the molecular biology of DNA. These developments are moving the investigation of nature closer to nurture. The second half of the chapter considers contemporary environmental theory and research that is moving the investigation of nurture closer to nature.

## Nature

In genetics, the word *nature* refers to what is typically thought of as inheritance. Inheritance denotes DNA differences transmitted from generation to generation. In 1865, Mendel noted the discrete inheritance of single-gene traits in pea plants, such as smooth versus wrinkled seeds. In contemporary human genetics as well, the focus is on genetic differences among individuals, such as genes for differences in eye color, not the vast majority of DNA that is the same for all members of our species.

The word *nature* in this context does not refer to the nature of the human species. It refers to Galton's use of the word to denote genetically instigated differences among individuals within the species. Evolutionary arguments about the adaptiveness of species-typical characteristics are not irrelevant and they certainly are beguiling. However, the links between such species-typical evolution and genetic sources of individual differences are much looser than is often assumed. Sociobiology (e.g., Wilson, 1975), evolutionary psychology (e.g., Buss, 1991), and developmental psychobiology (e.g., Harper, 1992) primarily address differences between species, although attempts have been made to incorporate individual differences (Dawkins, 1983; DeKay & Buss, 1992). Because the raw material of evolution is genetic variability, it is easy to make the mistake of assuming that evolution implies genetic variability within a species and vice versa. For example, the natural use of language in the human species may be hardwired by evolution for language acquisition to occur if the minimal environment encountered by our species during development, most notably, another language user, is present. If it is the case that our species is a natural language user, this does not imply that differences among individual members of the species in their facility with language are also genetic in origin. Individual differences in language acquisition could be entirely environmental in origin. The causes of average differences between species are not necessarily related to the causes of individual differences within groups. Moreover, characteristics that have been subject to strong directional selection will not show genetic variability because strong selection exhausts genetic variability. In other words, when genetic variability is found among individuals within our species for a particular trait, it is likely that the trait was not important evolutionarily, at least in terms of directional section. Although the two perspectives need to be brought closer together, this book focuses on genetic differences between individuals in a species rather than genetic differences between species.

In addition, the word *nature* is not synonymous with DNA. Many DNA events are not inherited. The most important of these are the changes in gene expression that occur in response to events in the intracellular and extracellular environment, a topic emphasized in this chapter. As this chapter moves into the gray area at the interface between genes and environment, it may be helpful to think about identical twins as a check on what is genetic in the sense of inheritance. Identical twins are identical for all genetic events coded in DNA at conception. To the extent that changes in the expression of DNA are brought about by environmental factors not controlled by DNA as it is inherited at conception, identical twins can differ. Changes of this type, although they involve DNA, are initiated by environmental factors. They are not inherited. It should be noted that this definition of environment as all noninherited factors is a far broader definition of the environment than is usually considered. Although it is easy to argue about the breadth of this definition, all definitions are arbitrary—it is only important that they be explicit and useful.

In this section, classical structural genes are briefly described, followed by more detailed consideration of regulator genes that engage in a dialogue with the environment. Two current evolutionary theories relevant to the interface between nature and nurture are then discussed. The section ends by returning to quantitative genetic theory and methods, which provide the empirical foundation for the rest of the book.

## DNA

The molecular mechanism for the laws of inheritance discovered by Mendel lies in the double helix of DNA. The steps of the spiral staircase comprise pairs of four nucleotide bases (adenine, thymine, cytosine, guanine) that can occur in any order on one side of the double helix. The other side of the double helix is fixed because adenine always pairs with thymine and cytosine always pairs with guanine.

The human genome consists of more than 3 billion nucleotide base pairs, just considering one member of each of the 23 pairs of chromosomes. When Watson and Crick reported the structure of DNA in 1953, they realized that this structure suggests a mechanism for the two major functions of genes, self-duplication and protein synthesis. DNA copies itself by unzipping in the middle of the spiral staircase, with each half forming its complement. Mitosis is the DNA duplication of all chromosomes that occurs in all nongonadal cells to produce offspring cells identical to the parental cell. In the gonads, meiosis also duplicates DNA but produces eggs and sperm that contain only one member of each pair of chromosomes. The egg fertilized by the sperm thus contains the full complement of 23 pairs of chromosomes.

The other major function of DNA is transcription and translation of the genetic code. The code was cracked in the 1960s: The hereditary message of DNA lies in three consecutive nucleotide bases, a sequence that codes for 1 of 20 amino acids. For example, a sequence of three adenine bases codes for the amino acid phenylalanine. The central dogma of DNA describes how this code is transcribed into messenger RNA, which moves outside the nucleus of the cell and is translated by ribosomes in the cell body into amino acid sequences that are the basic building blocks of proteins and enzymes.

## STRUCTURAL GENES

Genes that code for proteins and enzymes are called structural genes. They represent the foundation of classical genetics. For example, 50 years ago, mutational research on common bread mold, *Neurospora*, showed that each enzymatic step in normal metabolic sequences is under the control of a single gene, giving rise to the "one-gene, one-enzyme" hypothesis (Beadle & Tatum, 1941). The first single-gene disorders discovered in the human species such as phenylketonuria (PKU; Folling, Mohr, & Ruud, 1945) involved metabolic disorders caused by mutations in structural genes.

Structural genes are not conducive to thinking about the dialogue between genes and the environment because they are largely deaf to the environment. Structural genes do not change in response to the environment. Whenever they are transcribed, they crank out their gene product regardless of the environment. Of course, in a larger perspective, natural selection and structural genes carry on a loud conversation. And of course structural genes cannot have their effect in a vacuum—their functioning requires the cellular and extracellular environment in which the species evolved. Nonetheless, there is no back-and-forth dialogue between structural genes and the immediate environment of the individual.

Consider PKU, which, like most genetic diseases, is a recessive gene that escapes the scrutiny of natural selection more easily than a dominant gene. For an individual with a double dose of PKU alleles, this particular DNA sequence on both chromosomes is transcribed and then translated into a sequence of amino acids. In its normal (non-PKU) state, this sequence of amino acids is the enzyme phenylalanine hydroxylase, which converts phenylalanine to tyrosine. For the PKU allele, the amino acid sequence is slightly different and results in phenylalanine hydroxylase that does not work properly in converting phenylalanine to tyrosine. Phenylalanine levels in the blood rise as phenylalanine is ingested in a wide variety of foods, particularly meats. As phenylalanine builds up in the blood, it depresses the level of other amino acids, depriving the developing nervous system of needed nutrients. In this way, the PKU allele leads to severe mental retardation. We can change the environment to accommodate the gene (the well-known therapy for PKU is to reduce phenylalanine in the diet), but the gene does not change in its structure or function in response to the environment. Although most people still think about genetic effects in terms of structural genes like PKU, the vast majority of genes are not like this. Most genes code for products that bind with DNA itself and serve to regulate other genes. These so-called regulator genes communicate closely with the environment. The phrase *regulator gene* does not do justice to this communication process because the word *regulator* denotes one gene controlling another. What is interesting about these genes is their interplay with the environment.

The classic example of gene regulation is the *lac* operon model. It is a good starting point for considering the dialogue between nature and nurture.

## NATURE-NURTURE AT A MOLECULAR LEVEL: THE *LAC* OPERON MODEL OF GENE REGULATION

Most structural genes, including the gene for phenylalanine hydroxylase, are responsive to the environment both inside and outside of the cell because their transcription is controlled by regulator genes whose function is to respond to the environment. The first and still one of the best understood examples of gene regulation occurs in the single-celled bacterium *E. coli*. β-galactosidase is an enzyme that metabolizes lactose, a saccharine substance in milk that is a major energy source of the gut-dwelling *E. coli*. One simple evolutionary strategy for ensuring that lactose can be metabolized would have been to hardwire the gene that codes for this lactose-metabolizing enzyme so that it is constantly transcribed and translated regardless of lactose in the environment. This strategy would guarantee that the necessary enzyme would be present whenever the bacterium encounters lactose.

However, evolution seldom takes this simple but wasteful route. A bacterium produces about 700 different enzymes. If each of these enzymes were continuously pumped out, there would not be enough storage room inside the cell to accommodate them. Also, there is an energy cost in producing enzymes. Even for the lowly single-celled bacterium, natural selection has employed an alternative strategy that is responsive to the environment. Since the 1950s, it has been known that enzyme synthesis could be turned on or off by the presence of the lactose substrate. In a lactose-rich environment, E. coli contain thousands of β-galactosidase molecules. In contrast, when E. coli are placed in environments without lactose, there are just a few of these molecules. This responsiveness to the environment primarily involves transcription, the synthesis of messenger RNA. Messenger RNA in bacteria is short-lived, existing for only 2 to 3 minutes. The number of messenger RNA molecules of β-galactosidase in E. coli varies from 35 to 50 in a lactose-rich environment to less than one molecule on average in the absence of lactose.

Understanding how bacteria regulate the production of this enzyme in response to their environment led to a Nobel prize for Jacob and Monod. In 1961, they proposed a model, called the *operon* model, in which the product of one gene serves to regulate another gene in response to the environment. For lactose and the production of β-galactosidase, the operon system is called the *lac* operon (see Figure 1.1). The structural gene that codes for β-galactosidase consists of 3,510 nucleotide bases. Adjacent to this structural gene is a short sequence of 21 nucleotide bases that is an on-off switch. This switch, called the operator sequence (not a gene because it does not code for anything), determines whether the structural gene will be transcribed. The combination of the structural gene and the operator sequence was called an *operon* by Jacob and Monod. There are also short promoter regions close to the structural gene that guide the enzyme, polymerase, to initiate RNA transcription at precisely the right place.

The operon switch is thrown by the product of another gene, called a regulator gene, which is often far away from the operon. For β-galactosidase, the regulator gene consists of 1,041 nucleotide bases and codes for a product consisting of a sequence of 347 amino acids. This product, called a repressor, binds with the operator sequence of the structural gene. When this occurs, the

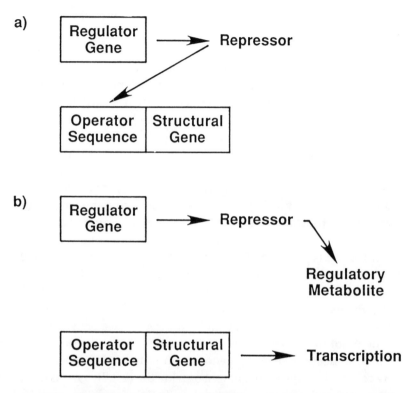

**Figure 1.1.** The operon model of gene regulation in the absence (panel a) or presence (panel b) of the regulatory metabolite (lactose in the case of the *lac* operon). In the absence of the regulatory metabolite, the repressor binds to the operator and the structural gene is not transcribed. When the regulatory metabolite is present, the repressor binds to it rather than to the operator, thus freeing the structural gene for transcription.

switch is turned off. That is, the repressor represses the operator sequence in the sense that transcription of the structural gene is inhibited. The key to the operon model is that this same repressor binds preferentially to lactose. When lactose is present, the repressor binds to lactose rather than to the operator sequence. This switches the operator sequence to the "on" position, which allows transcription of the structural gene. When all the lactose is metabolized, there are no more lactose molecules with which the repressor can bind. The repressor then binds with the operator sequence, shutting down the operon until lactose next appears. The story of regulation of β-galactosidase was found to be more complicated. Activation of the operon requires, in addition to freedom from repression, binding of cyclic adenosine monophosphate (cAMP) and a catabolite activator protein (CAP) to a region of the gene, called a promoter region, that is involved in the transcription process. This additional complexity illustrates the nature of regulatory systems even for this simplest example of the *lac* operon. Glucose regulates cAMP production. As glucose increases, cAMP decreases. As cAMP decreases, it disables CAP. CAP is needed to guide polymerase to transcribe the *lac* operon. Thus, in the presence of glucose, the *lac* operon can be turned off even when lactose abounds, which means that the operon is freed from lactose repression. This system thus preferentially metabolizes glucose before metabolizing lactose. An additional example of the systems nature of gene regulation is that the *lac* operon coordinates the expression not only of the β-galactosidase gene but also genes for a permease enzyme and a transacetylase enzyme.

The point of this example is to illustrate how, at the most basic level of molecular genetics, genes respond to environments. Lactose comes from the environment outside the cell. By means of the operon system of negative feedback and other regulatory systems, the β-galactosidase gene is transcribed to produce β-galactosidase only when it is needed, that is, when lactose is present.

GENE REGULATION IN MORE COMPLEX ORGANISMS

In organisms more complex than bacteria, mechanisms of gene regulation are much more diverse than the simple operon model (Maclean, 1989). For example, the transcription of many genes is modulated by so-called enhancer sequences that can greatly increase a gene's rate of transcription. These sequences are particularly interesting in the present context because their activity can be induced by environmental events such as heat shock, exposure to heavy metals, and viral infection (Gluzman & Shenk, 1984).

Unlike bacteria that are called prokaryotic because they have no nucleus, genes for eukaryotic organisms with nuclei are typically "split" genes. A split gene refers to DNA that contains segments, called introns, that are excised from "precursor" RNA that is initially transcribed from DNA. The remaining RNA segments (exons) are then spliced back together before this sliced and spliced messenger RNA leaves the nucleus for translation into amino acid sequences in the cell body. For example, the human β-globin gene includes 92 base pairs in its first exon, 138 in the first intron, 223 in the second exon, 889 in the second intron, and 123 in the third exon. Although the function of this complicated slicing and splicing process is not understood, introns may serve a regulatory function. It is known that different gene products can be coded by the same gene through alternative gene splicing, that is, splicing the RNA in different ways.

Some regulatory mechanisms have widespread effects on many genes. One example involves the small proteins called histones that combine with DNA to form the structure of chromosomes. Although histones were thought to do little more than to contribute to the structure of DNA, research now indicates that they initiate and repress transcription (Grunstein, 1992). Another example of far-reaching regulatory effects is hormones that modify the expression of diverse genes throughout the body. Hormones bind to cell receptors and then move through the cell to the nucleus where the hormone-receptor complex binds to DNA and participates in the regulation of transcription (Yoshinaga, Peterson, Herskowitz, & Yamamoto, 1992). Genes are also responsive to environments outside the body such as nutrition. The functioning of genes is also regulated by psychological environments. As you read this, you are changing rates of transcription of neurogenes involved in synthesis, storage, binding, and re-uptake of neurotransmitters and neuromodulators (Black et al., 1987).

In more complex organisms, it is especially apparent that genetic regulation is a system. For example, it is now widely accepted that gene expression is regulated by diverse transcription factors that bind to DNA and operate as a committee voting on the transcription of particular genes. A recent example involves bird songs. Songs similar to the species' song induce gene expression in the forebrain of canaries and zebra finches (Mello, Vicario, & Clayton, 1992). The gene that is induced by the relevant song codes for a transcription factor that regulates the transcription of other genes. This work is part of a major effort in neuroscience to investigate how experience regulates gene expression in neurons. For example, tweaking a rat's whiskers causes changes in gene expression in the sensory cortex (Mack & Mack, 1992). The picture that is beginning to emerge is one of a complex system of interacting transcription factors.

Although the preceding examples involve regulation of transcription of DNA into RNA, regulation can also occur after transcription. For example, the time it takes to degrade messenger RNA can be regulated, which affects the time the RNA is available for translation. Some regulation also occurs during the translation process. For example, messenger RNAs differ in the rate at which they are translated. Regulation even occurs after translation, as genes are involved in the sorting of proteins within cells and the delivery of proteins to their proper destinations.

For the present purpose, the details of gene regulation are less important than the general message: The products of many genes function in regulating the transcription and translation of other genes in response to the internal and external environment. It is now thought that much more genetic information is used to regulate, design, and to organize than to build (Lawrence, 1992). These examples of gene regulation help to demystify the interface between genes and environment at the molecular level by indicating mechanisms by which genes respond to environments.

GENE REGULATION AND DEVELOPMENT

Long-term developmental change is the key question of developmental biology. How do we begin life as a single cell and become an organism with trillions of cells with different functions even though each cell has the same DNA? The general answer is that DNA is turned on and off in different cell systems by longer term regulatory processes that may be similar to the short-term regulatory processes described in the preceding section.

Short-term regulatory mechanisms obviously require genetic adaptation to the environment, as in the example of the *lac* operon. However, it seemed reasonable to molecular biologists to suppose that the long-term control of development is not left to the vagaries of the environment. For this reason, they assumed that development is genetically programmed. Thus, in the 1970s developmental molecular biologists set out to find the genetic code for development, emulating research in the 1960s that discovered the genetic code by which structural genes are translated into polypeptides. Now, however, it is generally recognized that there are no genes that program the unfolding of development.

Sydney Brenner, who initiated developmental genetic research on the nematode roundworm, made this point well in a *Science* interview:

> At the beginning it was said that the answer to understanding of development was going to come from a knowledge of the molecular mechanisms of gene control. . . . I doubt whether anyone believes that anymore. The molecular mechanisms look boringly simple, and they don't tell us what we want to know. We have to try to discover the principles of organization, how lots of things are put together in the same place. I don't think these principles will be embodied in a simple chemical device, as it is for the genetic code. (Lewin, 1984, p. 1327)

To this I would add that the principles of organization involve a dialogue between genes and environment.

For example, a thousand complex molecules must be synthesized in a specific sequence during the half-hour life cycle of bacteria. It used to be assumed that this sequential synthesis was programmed genetically, perhaps by assembling the proper sequence of enzymes as a single coordinated unit so that component enzymes would pass efficiently from one step to another. There are in fact some genes whose gene products bind to DNA that are programmed to be expressed at specific times in development. Moreover, some genes are used and then are programmed to be reused to serve a different function later in development.

In general, however, the developmental sequence is not programmed in the genes. Evolution has not worried about making life easy for developmentalists by hardwiring neat sequential programs. Natural selection builds upon what is available and what works in the evolutionarily expected environment of the species at each step in development. The frequency of a mutant gene increases in a population if it has a positive effect on reproductive fitness in the complex context of all of the developmental interactions among other gene products of the organism. In this sense, development is not programmed in DNA. It is the jerry-built result of millions of small experiments to sculpt an efficient and effective reproducing organism in the context of the complicated systems of environments in which the species has evolved.

In other words, when the entire 3-billion base-pair sequence of nucleotide bases is known, it will not, in itself, tell us how development occurs. Development is the result of regulatory processes that involve a dialogue between genes and the intracellular and extracellular environment.

GENE REGULATION AND INDIVIDUAL DIFFERENCES

These examples of gene regulation focus on species-typical processes. What about individual differences in these processes? The short answer is that the origins of individual differences in these processes are not necessarily genetic even though gene regulation involves DNA. For example, environmental effects can easily account for differences among bacteria in lactose metabolism. Some bacteria encounter much more lactose than others, especially when the stomach in which they live belongs to an individual who consumes dairy products. If we assessed lactose metabolism of *E. coli* in the guts of several individuals, environmental variability could account for much of the observed variability among bacteria in the degree to which they metabolize lactose.

Genetic differences among bacteria can also affect differences in lactose metabolism. Because β-galactosidase is so vital to *E. coli*, mutational variations in the 3,510 nucleotide bases of the structural gene are not likely to survive natural selection, although such variability has not been carefully studied. Nonetheless, suppose that 1 of the 3,510 bases allowed a mutational substitution. The resulting β-galactosidase might be slightly more or less efficient in metabolizing lactose. This would lead to a genetic contribution to differences among bacteria in the degree to which they metabolize lactose. Another possibility is that a mutation in the regulator gene might alter the binding capability of the repressor, slightly affecting its ability to turn on and off the operator sequence of the structural gene.

Genetic contributions to individual differences in the lactose-metabolizing ability of bacteria can also accumulate from processes beyond the operon. For example, metabolism of lactose depends on the detection, capture, and transport of lactose molecules from the environment outside the cell. Some *E. coli* may be better at seeking out lactose in their environment and in making better use of it when they find it. Genetic effects on lactose-metabolizing ability include genetic variability in any of these components of the system, not just the structural gene or the regulator gene of the *lac* operon.

This simple example of gene regulation in a single-celled organism suggests a model of the interface between genes and environment for complex organisms as well. It shows how environments affect the function of genes. It also suggests how genes can affect experience. Genetic and environmental differences among bacteria can affect their ability to metabolize lactose and their ability to create a lactose-rich cellular environment by successful search, identification, capture, transport, and handling of lactose molecules. This attempt to eavesdrop on the dialogue between nature and nurture characterizes emerging research on genetic regulation.

The main message is that gene regulation has evolved, in all organisms but especially in complex organisms, to make genes responsive to the environment. In addition, genetic variability in regulatory processes results in differences in the way organisms use their environments. When specific genes are found that are responsible for genetic effects on experience, they are likely to be genes involved in regulation rather than structural genes.

SELECTION, INSTRUCTION, AND ADAPTATION

As mentioned earlier, initial work in developmental molecular genetics tried to find genetic programs coded in DNA that direct development. However, it is now recognized that nature and nurture play a duet. Going against this flow is an emerging theory in neuroscience that focuses on genetic programming. The theory is described in recent books by Gerald Edelman (1992) and Michael Gazzaniga (1992). This theory is called *selectionist* and it contrasts alternative views as *instructionist*. The essence of the selectionist argument is that what looks like instruction from the environment may be selection from built-in options.

The distinction between selection and instruction comes from immunology, where selectionist theory triumphed over the instructionist view. Antibodies are produced to neutralize antigens. Because there are at least a million different antibodies, more than the whole genome could possibly program, it was assumed that the body creates antibodies as somehow instructed by intruding antigens. Lymphocytes were thought to produce undifferentiated antibodies. When these meet an intruder molecule, they use the antigen as a template, folding around it, and neutralizing the antigen. The antibody's new configuration is locked in and the antigen is released so that other antibodies can be formed from it. The next time this reconfigured antibody meets the same type of antigen, its new configuration allows it to recognize the antigen quickly and to neutralize it.

Contrary to this instructionist hypothesis, it is now known that antibodies are selected from preexisting antibodies. First proposed at the turn of the century, selection theory was developed in its modern form more than 30 years ago (Burnet, 1959). Antibodies are receptors on lymphocyte cells, each of which codes for a specific antibody. Crucial to creating the needed diversity of antibodies is a hypervariable region of the antibody discovered by Edelman for which he won a Nobel prize in 1972 (Edelman, 1970). Genetic processes unique to genes of the immune system, such as recombination of gene segments and increased mutations, create this variability in DNA in the hypervariable regions of antibodies

(Leder, 1982). These processes create the billions of lymphocytes that produce diverse antibody receptors. The antibody receptors are sufficiently diverse to provide at least a rough match for any antigen structure. When an antigen interacts with the antibody receptor, the lymphocyte proliferates via mitosis to develop into a clone of cells each with the same antibody receptor. These progeny then secrete antibody molecules with the same binding capacity as the originator antibody receptor.

Thus instead of an instructional process in which new molecules are manufactured in response to the antigen, the immune response consists of a selection process in which an antigen selects from preexisting clones of cells. In addition, another selection process called hypermutation occurs when an antigen does not fit any antibody very well. A low-affinity binding causes the antibody's lymphocyte to proliferate but with greatly increased rates of random mutation. Some of the antibody's mutated descendants may bind more tightly to the antigen and thus neutralize it more effectively (French, Laskov, & Scharff, 1989). Although this seems more like an instructional process, hypermutation is genetically driven, randomly creating new antibodies that are then selected for their fit to the antigen. Thus, hypermutation as well as the basic immunological process of proliferation are best seen as examples of selection rather than instruction.

In 1967, Niels Jerne suggested that the brain might also develop via selection rather than instruction. Edelman's (1992) theory of neuronal group selection employs natural selection as a metaphor for the competitive selection of groups of neurons pruned by experience. Although Edelman's theory emphasizes environmental influence, it is a nativist theory in the sense that the environment merely prunes preexisting structures. Gazzaniga's book (1992) represents a more extreme selectionist theory that goes beyond neuronal selection to argue that the environment selects from a preexisting menu of capacities including "built-in knowledge systems" (p. 9):

> For the selectionist, the absolute truth is that all we do in life is discover what is already built into our brains. While the environment may shape the way in which any given organism develops, it shapes

it only as far as preexisting capacities in that organism allow. Thus, the environment selects from the built-in options; it does not modify them. (Gazzaniga, 1992, p. 3)

Gazzaniga emphasizes that, although strongly nativistic, this theory is more than an argument for innateness, that is, hardwired genetic programming impervious to the environment. Instead, the environment plays a role, albeit only in selecting from built-in options. He uses clothing as an example:

> In the instructional model, the tailor makes a suit to fit, whereas, in the selection model, the client goes to a large warehouse and picks out one that fits. (Gazzaniga, 1992, p. 91)

More explicitly, he argues:

> The strong form of the argument is that an organism comes delivered to this world with all the world's complexity already built in. In the face of an environmental challenge, the matching process starts, and what the outsider sees as learning is actually the organism searching through its library of circuits and accompanying strategies for ones that will best allow it to respond to the challenge. (Gazzaniga, 1992, p. 4)

Selectionist theory clearly bucks the trend of molecular genetics to move away from genetic programming toward a dialogue between nature and nurture. Although the immunology example of selectionist theory is impressive, it should be noted that none of the genetic tricks evolved by the immune system to meet the enormous demands of antibody structure and production has been shown to be used by other gene systems. Specifically, no such genetic mechanisms have been demonstrated in relation to brain structure and function. Because selectionist theory is attracting considerable attention, especially in the neurosciences, three other issues related to the theory warrant discussion.

*Selection, Species-Wide Themes, and Individual Differences.* The first issue concerns individual differences and their relation to selection of species-wide themes. Selectionists use the word *selection* to refer to two very different processes. The primary use of the word refers to selection of built-in options in the individual. This is not Darwinian selection in the sense of differences among individuals or kin that are selected on the basis of reproductive fitness. It is only secondarily that selection is used to connote Darwinian selection that builds these options into the species.

Concerning this evolutionary use of the word *selection*, selectionist theory, like other evolutionary theories, tends to be normative, focusing on species-wide universals of development. Gazzaniga, however, attempts to extend the selectionist argument to individual differences:

> Over the years there has been an inevitable tendency on the part of the critics to weaken selection theory by dismissing it as an aspect of what is innate. That way of thinking misses the point of the power of selection theory—its ability to account for the confounding variability of behavior. We all know that different animals respond differently to the same environmental challenge, and that animals of the same or similar genotype respond differently to varying environmental challenges. . . . In the case of the modern brain, a range of circuits that enable a variety of behavioral and cognitive strategies become matched with an environmental challenge and the selection process starts. (Gazzaniga, 1992, pp. 199-200)

The word *variability* is also being used in two ways: (1) differences between individuals ("different animals respond differently to the same environmental challenge") and (2) differences within individuals ("animals of the same or similar genotype respond differently to varying environmental challenges").

The nonevolutionary process of selection seems reasonable in relation to the second use of variability as within-individual selection of species-specific devices. However, the quotation has a very different implication in relation to differences between individuals: It implies that individual differences are environmental in origin. If "environmental challenges" are responsible for the process of selecting "circuits," it follows that differences among individuals are environmental in origin. That is, we all have the same circuits; the circuits activated for particular people depend on the environments they experience. However, this message about individual differences is confused because heritability is mentioned several times in Gazzaniga's book as if heritability provides support for the selectionist argument. As discussed earlier, the distinction between species-typical and individual-differences perspectives needs to be clearly maintained because explanations of one are not necessarily explanations of the other. Heritability is a within-species construct and does not provide support for the selectionist argument as stated. That is, if a built-in circuit is critical evolutionarily for a species, no genetic variability within the species will be tolerated—everyone will have this same circuit. Thus, if anything, evidence for heritability is contrary to the selectionist argument in its baldest form. Evidence for heritability is certainly contrary to the specific hypothesis that individual differences are completely environmental in origin.

*Semantic Issues.* Stretched too far from its solid foundation of the example of immunological selection, the selectionist argument degenerates into the truism that behavior requires a biological substrate. For example, Gazzaniga includes as support for his selectionist theory "the work of French Nobel laureate Jacques Monod, who, in the mid-1950s, showed that so-called adaptive enzymes are in fact induced by preexisting genes" (Gazzaniga, 1992, p. 3).

Gazzaniga implies that the *lac* operon model fits a selectionist model because there is a preexisting gene responsible for enzyme production. However, as discussed in the preceding section, the *lac* operon seems a better example of the instructionist position because the operon provides a mechanism for adapting to the environment. The operon changes its structure and function depending on the presence of lactose and glucose. If glucose is present or if lactose is present but glucose is not, the structural gene is freed for transcription. When the environment changes, the operon adapts by shutting down production of β-galactosidase. To argue that this is an example of selection because there is a preexisting genetic system leaves no room for any example of adaptation because all biological as well as behavioral functioning requires a biological substrate.

Another semantic issue is that selectionists exaggerate opposing positions by calling them "instructionist." This polemical trick conjures up images of Locke's tabula rasa. *Adaptation* seems to be a reasonable word to describe the dialogue between nature and nurture.

*Active Models of the Nature-Nurture Interface.* Instructionists and selectionists both have views of development that are too passive. For instructionists, the environment writes the score and conducts the performance as long as the orchestra members have the basic ability to play the music they are given. For selectionists, evolution is the composer and conductor, although the environment is allowed to audition some of the orchestra members. Neither extreme view does justice to the active transactions between the organism and its environment. This issue is well phrased in a review of Edelman's latest book:

> Substituting selectionist for instructional models of neural development and rejecting an information-processing model of how brains work, useful steps though they are, still fail to do justice to the brain as an active, dynamic, self-organizing system. Karl Popper has spoken of replacing what he sees as the "passive Darwinism" of sociobiology with an "active Darwinism" in which the actor, the organism, plays a part in the development of its own future. Edelman's selectionist metaphor in its passivity denies this possibility. (Rose, 1992, p. 427)

Chapter 5 returns to this topic.

THE EXTENDED PHENOTYPE

Another topic relevant to the duet between nature and nurture is Dawkins's (1983) concept of the extended phenotype. At a general level, the extended phenotype means that genes have functionally important consequences beyond the body of the organism. For example, if behavior is influenced genetically, behavioral artifacts such as nests can show genetic influence. Dawkins also considers extended effects of genes on other organisms, such as effects of parasites on their hosts or the effects of male pheromones on female physiology. More specifically, Dawkins is concerned with the level at which natural selection operates. His "central theorem" of the extended phenotype is that "an animal's behaviour tends to maximize the survival of the genes 'for' that behaviour, whether or not those genes happen to be in the body of the particular animal performing it" (p. 233). In this sense, Dawkins limits the use of extended phenotype to evolutionary adaptations. At this level of evolutionary theorizing, the concept of extended phenotype means something much more specific than the theme of this book, which is that genetic factors contribute to individual differences in experience. In one way, the message here is even more radical. Rather than examples such as parasites in which gene products of the parasite directly alter the host's physiology, this book considers much less direct links between genes and environment such as the response of other people to a child's genetic propensities or a child's creation of an environment correlated with its propensities.

## QUANTITATIVE GENETICS

This discussion of genetics has emphasized developments in molecular genetics and evolutionary genetics that consider the interface between nature and nurture. However, these approaches tend to focus on species-typical themes rather than within-species variations on these themes. In contrast, individual differences have always been the focus of quantitative genetics. Quantitative genetics was born 80 years ago to reconcile Mendelian (single-gene) genetics, which was only applicable to dichotomous disorders, and quantitative dimensions that characterize complex traits. The resolution to the problem was simple: Multiple genes, each operating according to the laws of heredity established by Mendel, together with environmental variation, will create continuous distributions. Methods of quantitative genetics—known as behavioral genetics when applied to behavior—include family, twin, and adoption designs and combinations of these that attempt to decompose observed variation for a trait into genetic and environmental components of variance. These methods assess the "bottom line" of genetic and environmental influences on phenotypes regardless of the developmental complexity of these effects. In terms of genetics, for example, quantitative genetic designs assess the bottom line of genetic effects on individual differences in development regardless of whether the effects are due to structural or regulator genes. (The methods of human quantitative genetics are discussed in Chapter 2.)

The label *quantitative genetics* is a misnomer because this theory and its methods are just as informative about the environment as they are about genetics. At the most basic level, quantitative genetic research documents the importance of environmental influences. It also suggests that the environment works differently than assumed in most theories of the environment from Freud's onward: Environmental factors that influence behavioral development largely operate to make children in the same family different from one another (Dunn & Plomin, 1990; Plomin & Daniels, 1987).

Quantitative genetics can take us beyond the basic nature-nurture question about "how much" variance can be attributed to genetic and environmental sources of variance. One example is development. Quantitative genetics can be used to investigate genetic and environmental influences on change and continuity in development (Plomin, 1986). Another example is the application of quantitative genetic approaches to investigate the environment in an attempt to illuminate the interface between nature and nurture. This is the theme of the rest of the book beginning with the next chapter. But before turning to quantitative genetic research on this topic, we consider what is known generally about nurture, again emphasizing new developments that are moving environmental theory and research closer to genetics.

## Nurture

For the environment, there is nothing comparable to the laws of heredity worked out by Mendel, to DNA, or to the triplet code. How is the environment transmitted and translated? What are the units of environment? Although much remains to be learned about genetics, understanding of genetic processes seems to be light years ahead of our understanding of environmental processes.

This second half of the chapter reviews current issues in environmental research from the perspective of genetics. The review focuses primarily on the psychological and developmental level of environmental analysis, relying heavily on a recent book in this series by Wachs (1992). It may be helpful, however, to begin by briefly considering what an analysis of the environment at the level of molecular biology might look like. Next, the history of environmental research at the psychological level of analysis is reviewed, followed by a discussion of models and levels of environment and development. Each of these topics points to the need to consider the environment as it interacts with an active organism that selects, modifies, and even creates its environment. This is the explicit message of several new environmental theories that are examined at the end of the chapter.

### MOLECULAR BIOLOGICAL ANALYSIS OF THE ENVIRONMENT

Thinking about a "molecular environment" analysis analogous to molecular genetic analysis can be illuminating. Just as genetics needs to be explained ultimately at the molecular level, the impact of the environment on the organism will also eventually need to be explained in terms of molecular regulatory processes. As discussed earlier in this chapter, lactose is the environmental unit for the *lac* operon. It is a molecule that is metabolized as a nutrient by bacteria. Even for this simplest case of environment, the lactose molecule serves as an environmental agent only when it interacts with the organism. Molecular biological analysis of lactose as an environmental agent must investigate how the molecule is detected by the bacterial cell, captured, transported, and metabolized. In this limited sense, molecular genetic analysis of the *lac* operon is also a molecular analysis of the environment, especially the interface between environment and organism. Lactose is simple because the molecule itself is the environmental agent. This is a far cry from environments at the psychological level of analysis such as the experience of reading a book. Such psychological environments are not incorporated physically into the organism's cells like lactose. Still, in the end (an end scarcely in imagination and certainly not in sight), we need to understand at a molecular biological level the perceptual, cognitive, and emotional processes by which experiences such as reading a book are encoded in the brain. In the meantime, molecular biological analyses of any level of environment in any organism will contribute conceptually to the psychological level of environmental analysis in at least two ways. First, it may help to sort out relevant categories of the environment. For example, if we could ever understand the biochemical pathways from an environmental event to a neural response, we could begin to sort out experiences on the basis of their neural pathways of response and lack of response. Second, molecular analyses of the environment are bound to lead to links with genetics, as in the example of the *lac* operon. Such findings will at the least stimulate more thought about the interface between nature and nurture at the psychological level of analysis.

HISTORY OF ENVIRONMENTAL RESEARCH

Three broad stages of environmental research in psychology can be distinguished (Bronfenbrenner & Crouter, 1983; Wachs, 1992). The goal of the first phase was to demonstrate the importance of environment in development without directly assessing the proximal environment of children. For example, developmental differences between children from different sociodemographic or cultural groups was interpreted as showing the importance of the environment.

The second historical phase of environmental research was driven by macrotheories such as Freud's psychoanalytic theory, Hebbs's neuropsychological theory, and cross-cultural theories. Theory guided research on specific aspects of the environment that might influence development (Wachs, 1992).

The third phase, which is still emerging, is characterized by a focus on processes, especially biological processes, by which environment is translated into development. This phase also shows greater awareness of the complexity of environmental influence, emphasizing different levels (Bronfenbrenner, 1989) and dimensions of the environment, moderation of environmental influence by other factors such as temperament (Wachs, 1992), longitudinal chains of causation (Rutter, 1989), and for some, constructivism, which, as discussed later, is especially relevant for thinking about the interface between nature and nurture.

Genetics can be considered in relation to each of these phases. To date, the focus of quantitative genetic research in the behavioral sciences has been on Phase I questions. That is, the relative importance of genetic and environmental influences on development has been examined using anonymous components of variance without measuring the environment directly. Quantitative genetic research has made an important but often overlooked contribution here: It provides the strongest available evidence for the importance of environmental influence. That is, twin and adoption studies usually find that more than half of the variance in behavioral development cannot be accounted for by genetic factors. For example, if identical twins are 40% concordant for schizophrenia, as recent studies suggest, no genetic explanation can account for the 60% discordance between these pairs of genetically identical individuals, given the current diagnosis of the disorder. Genetic research has also pointed to the importance of a neglected category of environmental influence, nonshared environmental influences that make children growing up in the same family different from one another (Dunn & Plomin, 1990; Plomin & Daniels, 1987).

Genetics was irrelevant in Phase II because the theories that guided the search for environmental influences during the heyday of environmentalism were largely environmental theories that ignored genetic influence.

Given its focus on developmental process, genetics has most to offer in relation to Phase III. Indeed, the theme of this book could be construed as an attempt to explore the genetic contribution to environmental research in Phase III. The key is to incorporate measures of the environment in genetic designs, especially multiple-level, multidimensional, developmentally sensitive measures of the environment that characterize Phase III environmental research.

## MODELS OF ENVIRONMENT

Another dimension along which the history of environmental research can be ordered reflects a general trend in developmental theory. Developmental models have moved away from viewing the child as a passive receptacle for environmental influences, to constructivist models in which children play an active role in selecting, modifying, and creating their own environments. In the passive model, the environment is viewed as a stimulus (S), something that happens to the individual. This model dominated research in Phases I and II. The active model could be called an organism-stimulus-response (O-S-R) model, although this label risks confusion with the connotations of S-O-R in learning theory. Here the emphasis is heavily on the "O," especially on the organism's active role in constructing environments. The O-S-R perspective is best captured by the word *experience*. This active model is compatible with the Phase III focus on transactional processes between the organism and its environment.

S and O-S-R models are so far apart that the middle ground warrants some consideration, even though this middle ground is not as clearly defined as the S and O-S-R extremes. For purposes of labeling, this middle ground can be called stimulus-response (S-R), although this label also runs the risk of being confused with learning theory.

These three perspectives on the environment have been discussed in relation to life events by Johnson (1986) and are outlined in Table 1.1. As usual in such classification schemes, the distinctions between S, S-R, and O-S-R models blur at their borders.

**TABLE 1.1**    Three Views of the Child's Environment

| | |
|---|---|
| Stimulus | What happens to the child; events independent of the child |
| Stimulus-Response | Response of the child is used as an index of what happens to the child |
| Organism-Stimulus-Response | What the child makes happen; child-driven events; experience |

However, the categories are useful in highlighting differences between environment and experience. The importance of the O-S-R approach is that it broaches the topic of the hyphen between nature and nurture, as discussed in Chapter 5. It is the reason why this book is called *Genetics and Experience*.

*Stimulus (S).* The most obvious way to think about the environment is as a stimulus, something that happens to the individual. Dictionary definitions denote environment as stimulus; its origins are in the word *environs*, which means "surroundings." Many measures of the environment in developmental research are of this type. Using life events as an example, parents are asked whether particular events occurred, such as change in financial state or change in residence. An example in the social sphere is parental control or discipline assessed independently of the child. Examples in cognitive and language research are parental education and parental vocabulary.

Despite the reasonableness of this environment-as-stimulus view, its major drawback is that the occurrence of such events, like lactose in the *lac* operon model, can have no effect on development unless they impinge on the child. Although Aunt Mabel's demise may loom as a major life event for the parent, the event may not even enter the world in which the child lives.

*Stimulus-Response (S-R).* The label *stimulus-response* denotes more than just a marker for the middle ground between the passive (S) and active (O-S-R) models. It includes attempts to assess the environment in relation to the child's responses. One of the best examples of an S-R approach comes from work on stress. Hans

Selye (1936) assessed chronic stress in terms of the individual's response, the General Adaptational Syndrome, rather than simply assessing threatening events. The typical developmental definition of the environment lies in this middle S-R part of the continuum: external stimuli that influence the individual. This definition implies that some response is assessed in addition to the stimulus itself.

How does the S-R model differ from the S and O-S-R models? Like the S model, the S-R model views the environment as a stimulus external to the individual. The S-R model differs from the S model in that the impact of the external stimulus is indexed by the individual's response. The difference between the S-R and the O-S-R orientation is one of degree rather than kind. The organism is, of course, required for a response in the S-R model. However, in contrast to the S-R model, the O-S-R model emphasizes the child's active selection, modification, and construction of environments.

For life events, the issue is not only that an event occurred, but also that the child knows that it occurred. This is important because parents' and children's reports differ even in relation to major life events and especially for more private events such as parental arguments or events at school (Rende & Plomin, 1991). Another example comes from a somewhat surprising quarter—investigations of the physical environment. *Affordance*, a concept derived from perception research, refers to objects that afford the child specific uses (Wachs, 1986) and is thus defined in terms of children's responses.

In the social arena, parental control and discipline assessed independently of the child was used above as an example of the S model. An S-R version is the assessment of children's compliance as an index of successful control and discipline. For cognition, parental education is an S example; children's attendance at preschool can be construed as an S-R example. For language, parental vocabulary is an S example and parental contingent vocalization can be considered as an S-R example in that it depends on the child's response.

Manipulative (experimental) studies can also be viewed in this light in that the stimulus is assessed in relation to its effect on average for an experimental group as compared to a control group.

Concerns about manipulative studies expressed in the developmental literature include representativeness, ecological validity, and generalizability (Bronfenbrenner, 1977; McCall, 1977; Wohlwill, 1973). In the present context, the important distinction is that manipulative experiments assume that the manipulation is functionally the same for all children. Individual differences within groups exposed to a particular environmental event are called error. This "error" includes person-by-treatment interactions that could be viewed in terms of individuals' modification and cognitive construction of the manipulation. Such individual differences in response to manipulation represent an important direction for future genetic research.

In summary, although this middle ground between S and O-S-R models is not as clearly defined as the extremes of the continuum, it includes much research that is neither independent of the child (the S model) nor focused on the organism's active transactions with the environment (the O-S-R model).

*Organism-Stimulus-Response (O-S-R).* In the O-S-R perspective, the "O" is something more than a black box in between "S" and "R." The organism actively selects, modifies, and even constructs environments. As Scarr (1992) has emphasized, people make their own environments. This view of environment as experience is compatible with the trend toward cognitive, constructivist interpretations in the behavioral sciences.

Using life events again as an example, the issue is not just that an event occurred (S) or that a child reports that it occurred (S-R). At the least, the O-S-R perspective asks the extent to which the child was upset by the event. The widely used Schedule of Recent Experiences (Holmes & Rahe, 1967) merely asked whether certain events occurred. More recent adaptations assess the impact of events (Sarason, Johnson, & Siegel, 1978).

In the stress literature, the O-S-R position is represented by Lazarus, who defines psychological stress as "a particular relationship between the person and the environment that is appraised by the person as taxing or exceeding his or her resources and endangering his or her well-being" (Lazarus & Folkman, 1985, p. 19).

Cognitive appraisal is key to this view of stress. Appraisal is involved in interpreting a situation and in evaluating one's resources in dealing with the situation. The same event could be appraised as a threat by one person and as a challenge by another. In an O-S-R approach, parental control and discipline could be assessed as a reaction to the child's behavior that calls for control and discipline. Farther out on the continuum than such reactive measures are measures that assess the child's active selection and creation of environments. For example, children differ in the degree to which they seek structure from their parents. In the cognitive realm, seeking information by asking "why" questions is an O-S-R example. Language development may provide the best general example of how children select and create their environments.

These examples indicate that the O-S-R view of the environment as active experience need not be limited to subjective measures such as questionnaires and interviews. Although much theorizing emphasizes an active model of development, few measures of the environment actually reflect this active model. For example, one of the most widely used environmental measures in cognitive development is the Home Observation for Measurement of the Environment (HOME; Caldwell & Bradley, 1978). The HOME is a semistructured interview consisting of 45 items, two thirds of which are based on observations in the home with the remainder based on parental reports. Most of the items assess the environment as stimulus, such as mothers' spontaneous vocalizations, naming of objects, and provision of toys and learning materials. A few items involve mothers' responses to the child such as "mother responds to child's vocalizations." The only HOME item that at least indirectly assesses the child's experience is how often the mother spends time with the child with books.

A need clearly exists for measures of experience. The results described in the next two chapters that show a genetic contribution to measures of the environment take on added significance in this light. Extant measures of the environment are largely measures of the environment as stimulus. Presumably such measures are at most a dull and unintended reflection of children's active interaction with the environment. Yet these measures yield evidence for significant genetic influence. It seems reasonable to predict that O-S-R measures of experience will show even greater genetic influence.

## LEVELS OF ENVIRONMENT

The environment can also be usefully considered in terms of different levels. For developmentalists, the most well-developed and influential model of levels of environment is the ecological model of Urie Bronfenbrenner (1989). The model consists of four levels. The *microsystem* involves proximal interactions that directly involve the child. The *mesosystem* is a system of microsystems in the sense that developmental effects involve interactions among microsystems such as home and school. The *exosystem* refers to interactions between settings in which at least one setting does not directly involve the child, such as interactions between the home and the parents' workplace. The *macrosystem* refers to the overall system of microsystems, mesosystems, and exosystems that characterize a culture or subculture. The model emphasizes that interactions can occur between and within levels.

Psychologists tend to study microsystems while sociologists and anthropologists are more interested in exosystems and macrosystems. In relation to genetics, the proximal processes of microsystems that directly involve the child are more likely to reflect genetic influence than are the global and diffuse environmental levels of exosystems and macrosystems. For this reason, this book focuses on environments and experiences at the level of microsystems. Nonetheless, genetic influence can be considered at higher levels. For example, in Chapter 3, evidence is reviewed for genetic influence on social support and on work environment. It is interesting that these exosystem measures show some genetic influence, although perhaps less than microsystem measures such as parenting. Measures at the exosystem level might be affected by genetically influenced characteristics of the individual such as intelligence and personality and could thus be found to affect development via nature in addition to nurture.

Although genetic methods are certainly better equipped to explore genetic contributions to individual differences than to average group differences, even macrosystems cannot be assumed to be devoid of genetic effects. For example, Kagan and his colleagues have recently suggested that genetically based differences between Asian and Caucasian infants in ease of arousal to stimulation may contribute to differences in the classic philosophies of Asians and Europeans (Kagan, Arcus, & Snidman, 1993). Another example is that genetic effects on attitudes can contribute to global environmental issues (Eaves, Martin, & Eysenck, 1989).

*Relations Among Levels.* An area of current environmental research is the issue of relationships among levels of environment (e.g., Bronfenbrenner, 1989; Wachs, 1992). In psychological research, this research thrust can be seen primarily in investigations of the relationship between parental beliefs and behavior on the one hand and culture, work environment, and stress on the other. For example, parenting is clearly related to cultural norms (e.g., Goodnow, 1988). Work environments and stress also relate to parenting (Belsky, 1984; Crouter & McHale, 1993). It is possible that genetic factors contribute to some links between levels.

*Interactions Among Levels.* Recent reviews have noted that associations between microenvironmental processes and development might interact with macroenvironmental parameters (Bronfenbrenner, in press; Wachs, 1991). For example, several examples suggest that environment-outcome associations differ in different ethnic groups. Japanese mothers talk to their infants to soothe them, whereas American mothers more often talk to their infants to stimulate them (Caudill & Weinstein, 1969). Measures of home environment relate to cognitive development to a greater extent in black and in white families than in Mexican-American families (Bradley et al., 1989). Similarly, adolescents' perceptions of parenting are associated with school achievement to a greater extent for black and white children than for Asian-American children (Dornbush, Ritter, Leiderman, Roberts, & Fraleigh, 1987).

Mesosystem variables can also mediate microenvironment—development relationships. Parenting relates to children's development less for children in day care than for children not in day care (Howes, 1990). Home environment relates more strongly to children's verbal ability before children go to school rather than when they are in school (Luster & Dubow, 1991).

Interactions among levels of environment have not been considered in genetic analyses of developmental outcomes, of environmental measures, or of environment-development associations. This is an important direction for future genetic research. A note of caution, however, is that detection of such interactions requires large samples because they essentially require testing for differences in correlations between groups. A focused search among extreme groups likely to show such interactions may be the most efficient strategy (Wachs & Plomin, 1991).

ENVIRONMENTAL SPECIFICITY

As reviewed by Wachs (1992), environmental research has moved beyond the study of associations between global environments (such as SES) and global outcomes (IQ). Specificity is the hallmark of more recent research—different aspects of the environment are assumed to relate to different aspects of development. For example, environmental studies in the past assessed a single good-bad dimension of the home environment. The HOME, mentioned earlier, is multidimensional and shows that parental involvement and provision of play materials predict subsequent cognitive development, whereas caregiver acceptance and use of negative control do not (Bradley et al., 1990). Specificity is the logical outcome of the fact that both environment and development are multidimensional in nature (Wachs, 1992).

For example, one could argue for the use of a total HOME score because factor analysis of the HOME items reveals a general factor (first unrotated principal component) in addition to the separate factors seen in factor rotations. However, the correlational structure of the HOME items considered by themselves is a different issue from the ability of these items to predict development. That is, although a case can be made for a general composite or total score based on psychometric considerations, this is not necessarily the best dimension for predicting different aspects of development. The most sensible approach may be to include both general and specific factors of the environment in a multiple regression framework in order to determine whether specific factors add predictive power beyond that of the general factor.

A cautionary note is that specificity requires significant differences in associations, and such significance has rarely been tested. Another concern is that the banner of specificity and multidimensionality may produce a welter of nonreplicable results (Belsky, 1990).

ENVIRONMENTS ACROSS TIME

Environments are not static. They change across time, especially environmental measures that are sensitive to developmental changes in the child (Wachs, 1992).

Of central interest in earlier environmental studies was the question of whether children are especially sensitive to environmental influences at certain times in development (Bornstein, 1989; Colombo, 1982). However, evidence for such sensitive periods is weak, perhaps because it is a difficult issue to address rigorously (Bornstein, 1989). A related issue is the long-term effect of early environment. Some researchers argue that early experiences are disproportionately important (e.g., Wachs & Gruen, 1982), but others disagree (e.g., Clarke & Clarke, 1989). A compromise position is that early experience is particularly effective when it continues to have a cumulative effect on development (Hanson, 1975). It has recently been suggested that research in part supports all three views (Wachs, 1992). One of the few studies that explicitly tested the three models found support for all three models, depending on the outcome and environmental variables chosen for analysis (Bradley, Caldwell, & Rock, 1988).

NEW ENVIRONMENTAL THEORIES
OF NATURE AND NURTURE

The most promising sign that environmental psychology is moving toward genetics is the appearance of new nature-nurture theories by leaders in the environmental field: Bronfenbrenner and Ceci (1993), Horowitz (1993), and Wachs (1992, 1993). Although these environmental researchers are by no means in complete agreement with the theories and methods of quantitative genetics, nor do they use quantitative genetic strategies in their research, each has proposed an environmental theory that attempts to encompass genetic factors. The common theme in the "bio-ecological model" of Bronfenbrenner and Ceci, Horowitz's "comprehensive new environmentalism," and Wachs's "multi-determined probabilistic systems framework" is the need to address Anastasi's (1958) question of how genotypes and environments interact in development.

The "bio-ecological model" of Bronfenbrenner and Ceci (1993) is most developed as a testable theory. Central to the theory is the concept of proximal process:

> Especially in its early phases, and to a great extent throughout the life course, human development takes place through processes of progressively more complex reciprocal interaction between an active, evolving bio-psychological human organism and the persons, objects, and symbols in its immediate environment. To be effective, the interaction must occur on a fairly regular basis over extended periods of time. Such enduring forms of interaction in the immediate environment are referred to henceforth as *proximal processes*. (p. 317, italics in original)

Proximal processes are seen as the means by which genotypes become phenotypes:

> Genetic potentials for development that exist within human beings are not merely passive possibilities but active dispositions expressed in selective patterns of attention, action, and response. (p. 316) . . . Among the most consequential *person* characteristics affecting the

form, power, content, and direction of proximal processes is genetic inheritance. (p. 318, italics in original)

The concrete example used by Bronfenbrenner and Ceci involves the relationship between mother-child interaction and behavioral problems as a function of social class. This example represents organism-environment interactions across levels of environment. The authors predict that heritability differs across the groups. Specifically, they predict that heritability "will be greater when levels of proximal process are high and smaller when such processes are weak" (p. 320). However, one could argue that if proximal processes are "high" this implies that environmental influences are greater, which suggests that heritability should be lower, not higher, when levels of proximal process are high (Wachs, personal communication, February 17, 1993).

Research on such genotype-environment interactions represents an important direction for Phase III research on the environment. For example, it would be interesting if research were to show that heritability of behavioral problems is higher (or lower) when mother-child interaction is good. However, it is less clear how research on genotype-environment interactions addresses the "progressively more complex reciprocal interaction between an active, evolving bio-psychological human organism and the persons, objects, and symbols in its immediate environment" (Bronfenbrenner & Ceci, 1993, p. 317). The concept of genotype-environment correlation, discussed in Chapter 4, seems better suited to this goal.

The papers by Bronfenbrenner and Ceci, Horowitz, and Wachs also discuss barriers to communication and collaboration between environmentalists and geneticists, as do recent papers by behavioral geneticists (e.g., Goldsmith, 1993; Rowe & Waldman, 1993; Rutter, Silberg, & Simonoff, 1993). The general consensus is that abstract arguments are unlikely to resolve the complicated issues at the interface of nature and nurture. What is needed is research collaboration "to construct actual empirical bridges between nature and nurture" in which environmentalists and geneticists are full and equal partners (Wachs, 1993, p. 388).

## Summary

Research and theory in genetics (nature) and in environment (nurture) are beginning to converge. Although there is still a very long way to go, the common ground is a model of active organism-environment interaction in which nature and nurture play a duet rather than one directing the performance of the other. It seems clear that some of the most interesting questions for genetic research involve the environment and some of the most interesting questions for environmental research involve genetics. For this reason, genetic studies should include measures of the environment that capitalize on the multiple-level, multidimensional, developmentally sensitive advances of "Phase III" environmental research. For this same reason, environmental research should make use of genetic designs, especially in research on family environment where family members are genetically related in order to disentangle genetic and environmental sources of familial resemblance.

The next chapter begins the empirical examination of one corner of this world at the hyphen in the phrase *nature-nurture*. In the next two chapters, quantitative genetic methods are applied to measures of familial (Chapter 2) and extrafamilial (Chapter 3) environment. Widespread genetic effects have been found for such measures. Chapter 4 considers factors that might mediate this genetic contribution to environmental measures. Chapter 5 summarizes the themes of this book in the form of a theory of genetics and experience.

# 2

# The Nature of Nurture

*Family Environment*

Chapter 1 showed that genetic and environmental theory and research are evolving toward one another. The core of this book is an empirical phenomenon discovered during the past decade in which nature and nurture have come together. This is the finding that genetic factors contribute to measures widely used as measures of the environment. Even though the first research on this topic was published just a decade ago, more than a score of quantitative genetic studies using various genetic designs and measures have converged on the conclusion that genetic differences among individuals contribute to measures of the environment.

## Quantitative Genetic Methods

Space does not permit a detailed presentation of the quantitative genetic methods upon which this research is based, but a brief discussion is necessary for readers unfamiliar with this approach. Human quantitative genetic research relies on family, adoption, and twin designs. Family studies of human behavior assess the extent to which genetically related individuals living together resemble each other. Such studies cannot disentangle possible environmental sources of resemblance. Separating genetic and environmental sources of familial resemblance is the point of adoption studies. Genetically related individuals adopted apart give evidence of the extent to which familial resemblance is the result of hereditary resemblance. The most dramatic evidence of genetic influence is the study of adopted-apart identical twins. Results from the Minnesota Study of Twins Reared Apart will be discussed at several points in this book (Bouchard, Lykken, McGue, Segal, & Tellegen, 1990). The environmental side of the adoption design is equally powerful: The resemblance of genetically unrelated individuals adopted together directly assesses the extent to which familial resemblance is due to shared family environment.

Twin studies also provide a kind of natural experiment in which the resemblance of identical twins, whose genetic relatedness is 1.0, is compared to the resemblance of fraternal twins, first-degree relatives, whose genetic relatedness is .50. If heredity affects a trait, identical twins should be more similar for the trait than fraternal twins. Much of the research to be discussed, especially the early research, involves this classical twin design that compares the resemblance of identical and fraternal twins.

As in any quasi-experimental design, these methods have possible problems, most notably the equal environments assumption for the twin method and selective placement for the adoption method. However, these are empirical issues and research suggests that these are not major problems. Moreover, the assumptions of the twin method are very different from the assumptions of the adoption method and yet the two methods generally converge on the conclusion that genetic effects are important.

Most research now combines the power of the various approaches. Three such combination studies are mentioned frequently in this book. The first is the Colorado Adoption Project (CAP), which combines the adoption and family designs (DeFries, Plomin, & Fulker, in press). Launched in 1975, the CAP is a longitudinal adoption study that studied the children, parents (including the biological parents of adopted-away children), and home environments of 245 adoptive families and 245 matched nonadoptive families when the children and their younger siblings were 1, 2, 3, and 4 years of age. The children were subsequently studied in the laboratory at 7 years of age, and administered telephone tests and interviews at 9 and 10 years. The parent-offspring design includes "genetic" relationships (biological parents and their adopted-away children), "environmental" relationships (adoptive parents and their adopted children), and "genetic-plus-environmental" relationships (nonadoptive parents and their children). The CAP sibling adoption design includes nonadoptive siblings (biological siblings reared together in nonadoptive families) and adoptive siblings (genetically unrelated children reared in the same adoptive homes).

Another combination design frequently mentioned in this book is the Swedish Adoption/Twin Study of Aging, which is a study of older individuals (SATSA; Pedersen et al., 1991). The SATSA design combines the classical twin comparison of identical (MZ) and fraternal (DZ) twins reared together (MZT, DZT) and an adoption design that includes both MZ and DZ twins reared apart (MZA, DZA) with a total of about 700 twin pairs. The third combination design is the Nonshared Environment in Adolescent Development (NEAD) project, which involves a national sample of 719 two-parent families with same-sex adolescent siblings (Reiss et al., 1994). The design includes six groups of siblings: nondivorced families with MZ twins, DZ twins, and full siblings, and stepfamilies with full siblings, half siblings, and genetically unrelated siblings. This novel design includes siblings whose genetic relatedness varies from 1.0 (MZ twins) to .50 (DZ twins and full siblings) to .25 (half siblings) to .00 (genetically unrelated siblings).

Family, adoption, and twin studies and combinations of these designs can be used to estimate the magnitude of genetic effects as well as their statistical significance. This is the descriptive statistic called heritability. Heritability is an estimate of effect size given a particular mix of existing genetic and environmental factors in a particular population at a particular time. It is a descriptive statistic that estimates the proportion of phenotypic variance (i.e., individual differences in a population, not behavior of a single individual) that can be accounted for by genetic variance. It describes "what is" rather than predicting "what could be" or "what should be." Heritability does not imply genetic determinism—it refers to probabilistic propensities, not predetermined programming.

Consider height. Correlations for first-degree relatives are about .45 on average, whether relatives are reared together or adopted apart. Identical and fraternal twin correlations are .90 and .45, respectively, regardless of whether they are reared together or adopted apart. These results indicate significant genetic effects. For these height data, heritability is estimated as 90%. This estimate of effect size indicates that, of the differences among individuals in height in the populations sampled, most of the differences are due to genetic rather than environmental differences among individuals.

Rather than estimating heritability in a piecemeal manner from multiple-group comparisons (such as the SATSA design, which includes identical and fraternal twins reared together and twins reared apart), model-fitting has become standard because model-fitting analyzes all of the data simultaneously, tests a model, makes assumptions explicit, provides maximum-likelihood parameter estimates and standard errors of the estimates, and permits tests of alternative models. (See Loehlin, 1992b, for an introduction to quantitative genetic model-fitting, and see Neale and Cardon, 1992, for greater detail.) Most of the heritability estimates presented in this book were derived from such model-fitting analyses. Details concerning quantitative genetic methods and their application to behavior are also available elsewhere (Plomin, DeFries, & McClearn, 1990).

These same methods have been applied to many behavioral traits in the domains of cognitive abilities, personality, and psychopathology (see Plomin & McClearn, 1993, for a recent review). The point of this chapter and the following chapter is that these methods can also be applied to the analysis of environmental measures considered as dependent variables. The findings from such research have been quite surprising.

## Rowe's Studies

In 1980, I was asked to review a manuscript for *Developmental Psychology* that was written by David Rowe. Rowe was beginning his last 2 years of graduate school when I took my first position at the University of Colorado at Boulder in 1974, and we published several papers together. Although he was more of a former colleague than a former student, at first I did not think that I would review the manuscript because of the appearance of a conflict of interest. However, when I read the manuscript, I was excited by its creative idea. Because I thought that the novelty of the paper might create trouble in the review process, I decided to submit a review after noting my possible bias. It was good that I did so because the other review began with the sentence, "The trouble with this paper is that the author's logic is faulty," which captures the tone of the review. My review began "I find this research creative and novel. The idea of studying perceived environment from a behavioral genetics perspective is exciting and the results are quite interesting."

The manuscript was entitled, "Environmental and Genetic Influences on Dimensions of Perceived Parenting: A Twin Study" (Rowe, 1981). It reported the results from a relatively small sample (89 pairs) of adolescent twins who were administered a self-report questionnaire. Expressed this way, the study was not at all novel because scores of such twin studies have been reported, primarily for self-report measures of personality. What was creative was the particular measure used. It was a questionnaire not about personality but about perceived parenting, a measure usually employed as a measure of family environment. Such measures of family environment are often correlated with children's development and such associations are then usually interpreted causally in terms of environmental influence.

Why would anyone want to conduct a twin analysis of a measure of the family environment? In a follow-up paper, Rowe explained:

A novel approach to the study of the home environment is to model environmental treatments using behavioral genetic methods. The "environment" that is experienced by a child is certainly not a phenotypic characteristic of the child in the traditional sense of a measurable trait. The type of environment a child experiences is the result of a long history of parent-child interaction that involves both characteristics of the parent and of the child. However, when the environment is measured independently for each child in a family, behavioral genetic approaches are applicable to it. The environment of sibling A can be correlated with the environment of sibling B. (Rowe, 1983, p. 416)

If genetic factors play no role in the environmental measure—which is what one would expect if it is truly a measure of the environment independent of the organism—the correlation for identical twins should be similar in magnitude to the correlation for fraternal twins. This was the case for two dimensions of parental control assessed in Rowe's study. The measure used was an abbreviated version of Schaefer's Children's Reports of Parental Behavior Inventory (Schaefer, 1965). Similar to most measures of parenting, broad factors emerged from factor analyses that represent two major dimensions of parenting: control (e.g., permissiveness, organization) and warmth (e.g., affection, supportiveness). Rowe found two control dimensions that he referred to as *control-autonomy* and *firm-lax control*, and he called his warmth factor *acceptance-rejection*.

The results of Rowe's study are summarized in Table 2.1. For the control-autonomy dimension, the identical (MZ) and fraternal (DZ) twin correlations were .44 and .47 when the twins rated their mother and .43 and .46 when they rated their father. The other control dimension, firm-lax control, showed similar results. MZ and DZ correlations were .55 and .46 for ratings of mother and .43 and .45 for ratings of father. Two aspects of these results are interesting. First, siblings, in this case twins, perceive their parents' treatment of them as only moderately similar. It might surprise some readers to see the extent to which siblings perceive their parents as treating them differently. This raises the important topic of nonshared environment—why siblings in the same family are so

**TABLE 2.1**   Twin Correlations for Adolescent Twins' Ratings of Their Parents' Child Rearing

| | Twin Correlations | |
| --- | --- | --- |
| *Measure* | MZ | DZ |
| *Children's Reports of Parental Behavior* | | |
| *Perception of Mother:* | | |
| Acceptance-rejection | .54 | .17* |
| Control-autonomy | .44 | .47 |
| Firm-lax control | .55 | .46 |
| *Perception of Father:* | | |
| Acceptance-rejection | .74 | .21* |
| Control-autonomy | .43 | .46 |
| Firm-lax control | .43 | .45 |
| *Family Environment Scales* | | |
| Acceptance-rejection | .63 | .21* |
| Restrictiveness-permissiveness | .44 | .54 |

SOURCE: Adapted from Rowe (1981, 1983). A similar version of this table appeared in Plomin, R., & Bergeman, C. S. (1991). The nature of nuture: Genetic influence on "environmental" measures. *Behavior and Brain Sciences, 14,* 373-427. Reprinted with permission of Cambridge University Press.
NOTE: The results for the Children's Reports of Parental Behavior Inventory are reported in Rowe (1981) for a sample of 89 twin pairs. Results for the Family Environment Scales were reported by Rowe (1983) in a study of 90 pairs of twins.
* MZ correlation significantly ($p < .05$) greater than DZ correlation.

different, a topic to be discussed later—and suggests that differential perceptions of parental treatment may be part of the answer. More to the immediate point is the second aspect of these findings. Because the MZ correlations are no greater than the DZ correlations, individual differences in adolescents' perceptions of parental control cannot be attributed to genetic factors. Sibling similarity in ratings of parental control is due to shared environmental factors (not shared heredity), which is not surprising because the two children in each family are rating the same mother and the same father.

The pattern of twin correlations for the warmth scale contrasted sharply with the results for the control scales. The MZ and DZ correlations were .54 and .17 for ratings of mothers' warmth and .74 and .21 for ratings of warmth of fathers. Despite the relatively small sample size, the MZ correlations were significantly greater than the DZ correlations for both mothers and fathers, suggesting a genetic contribution to adolescents' perceptions of their parents' warmth. It should be emphasized that these results also provide evidence for nongenetic influence, as indicated by MZ correlations less than 1.0. However, it is not news to show that environmental measures are environmental; the news is that genetic factors contribute to environmental measures.

What does this finding of a genetic contribution to adolescents' perceptions of parental warmth mean? The question is central to this book and merits a careful and lengthy answer. However, the short answer is that some genetically influenced processes may be involved in adolescents' reports of their parents' warmth. Perhaps attributional processes underlying self-reported perceptions are a manifestation of genetic influence. Perhaps the genetic contribution is not just in the eye of the beholder. It might be in the behavior of the child to which the parent responds. As discussed in Chapter 4, the question of the processes responsible for the genetic role in measures of the environment provides an empirical point of entry into the hyphen between nature-nurture.

Before going too far toward interpretation, the basic phenomenon of a genetic role in measures of the environment needs better documentation. The article by Rowe was just one small twin study that suggested genetic effects for one of three scales. Perhaps it was a fluke.

In 1983, Rowe published a second article that repeated the 1981 study and extended it. The study included an independent sample of 90 pairs of adolescent twins and a different measure of the family environment. The measure was the widely used Family Environment Scale (Moos & Moos, 1981), which assesses the general atmosphere of the family rather than specific parenting practices. Two second-order factors emerged that represent the control and warmth dimensions typically found in studies of parenting. Rowe labeled the two dimensions *restrictiveness-permissiveness* and *acceptance-rejection*.

The results, also included in Table 2.1, clearly replicated those of the first study. For the control dimension, the MZ and DZ correlations were .44 and .54, respectively. This pattern of twin correlations suggests no heritability and moderate effects of shared environment. In contrast, the warmth dimension yielded MZ and DZ correlations of .63 and .21. The MZ correlation is significantly greater than the DZ correlation and thus implicates genetic factors. The 1983 report also included analyses of 118 pairs of non-twin siblings from another study. The use of non-twin siblings tests the generalizability of twins to non-twin siblings. For example, perhaps twins, who are exactly the same age, may be treated more similarly than non-twin siblings, who are a year or more apart in age. To the contrary, the sibling correlations were similar to, even somewhat higher than, those for DZ twins: .59 for control and .46 for warmth. This finding suggests that the twin results can be generalized to non-twin siblings.

## Other Research on Children's Perceptions of Family Environment

It is rare in the behavioral sciences to see such perfect replication of a new and exciting finding. The extent of the replication in these two studies with different subjects and different measures was to some extent due to luck because the relatively small sample sizes of these two studies yielded twin correlations with large standard errors. Additional replication was needed with larger samples. It was also important to see whether similar results would emerge from studies using non-twin subjects, ages other than adolescence, and measures other than questionnaire ratings of parenting.

Before turning to studies that explicitly addressed this issue, it is possible to reinterpret some older studies in this new light. The earliest relevant research was not conducted for the purpose of investigating a genetic contribution to measures of the family environment. The goal of the research was to address the "equal environments" assumption of the twin method by studying whether MZ twins are treated more similarly than DZ twins (Lehtovaara, 1938; Loehlin & Nichols, 1976; Smith, 1965; Wilson, 1934; Zazzo, 1960). Although MZ twins were found to be treated more similarly by their parents for some measures, the general conclusion from such research has been that such MZ-DZ differences in treatment do not relate environmentally to twin differences in the behaviors under investigation (Plomin, DeFries, & McClearn, 1990). For example, within MZ twin pairs, twin pairs treated more similarly were not found to be more similar on behavioral traits (Loehlin & Nichols, 1976). Another set of studies showed that, for twins whose zygosity is mistaken by their parents, true zygosity rather than mistaken zygosity is related to twin similarity (Goodman & Stevenson, 1991; Scarr, 1968; Scarr & Carter-Saltzman, 1979). Thus, labeling twin pairs as MZ or DZ does not seem to be an important source of unequal environments.

However, the issues are more complex than is commonly recognized. This research literature assumed that treatment of MZ and DZ twins is strictly an environmental affair. If genetic factors contribute to environmental measures, we would expect MZ twins to be more similar than DZ twins. Is this not a violation of the equal environments assumption? Although it might seem so, the answer is "no." The equal environments assumption of the twin method refers to the environmental component of variance, that is, the effects of environmental influences on individual differences for a trait. However, the genetic contribution to measures of the environment should not be considered part of the environmental component of variance nor the genetic component of variance because it is a combination of the two. It involves a different component of variance called genotype-environment correlation, discussed in Chapter 4. The issues are certainly broader than the equal environments assumption of the twin method because other designs such as adoption studies also furnish evidence for genetic effects on measures of the environment. Evidence from non-twin designs are reviewed in the following sections.

RETROSPECTIVE REPORTS OF MIDDLE-AGED TWINS REARED APART AND TWINS REARED TOGETHER

Five years after Rowe's second report, his results were replicated and extended in a study that was part of the Swedish Adoption/Twin Study of Aging (SATSA; Plomin, McClearn, Pedersen,

Nesselroade, & Bergeman, 1988). An abbreviated version of the FES (Family Environment Scales) was completed by 179 reared-apart twin pairs and 207 reared-together pairs. In addition to its powerful design, the SATSA study was novel in that the twins were 60 years old on average. These middle-aged twins were asked to report retrospectively about the environment of the family in which they were reared half a century earlier. The FES was modified for this purpose. It should be noted that even though the twins were middle-aged, the design involves their perceptions of the family environment in which they were reared. Although the accuracy of retrospective reports of parenting can be doubted (Halverson, 1988), adults' memories or even myths about their parents are part of their perceived experience.

In addition to presenting results for the second-order factors of the FES, eight of the primary FES scales were analyzed, and this proved illuminating as shown in Table 2.2. Focusing on the direct estimate of heritability provided by MZA, the lowest correlation (−.03) is for the FES primary Control scale. This low correlation for MZA indicates no genetic influence for perceptions of parental control. Although the classical twin comparison of MZT and DZT suggests some heritability, model-fitting analyses that analyze data from all four groups simultaneously yield the lowest heritability estimate for this scale ($h^2 = .15$). This replicates Rowe's finding concerning adolescents' perceptions of parental control. The new finding was that analysis of the primary FES scales indicated that it is not just warmth that shows a genetic contribution but most of the scales other than control. Model-fitting analyses yielded significant genetic estimates for the following FES scales: Expressiveness, Conflict, Achievement Orientation, Intellectual-Cultural Orientation, Active-Recreational Orientation, and Organization.

The results for the second-order FES scales are presented at the bottom of Table 2.2. Similar to Rowe's findings, genetic effects were nonsignificant for a second-order control dimension called System Maintenance ($h^2 = .11$). This dimension comprises the Control and Organization primary scales. In contrast, heritability was significant ($h^2 = .38$) for a second-order warmth dimension called Relationship that consists of the Cohesion, Expressiveness,

**TABLE 2.2** Twin Correlations and Heritabilities for Adult Twins' Retrospective Ratings of Their Childhood Family Environment

| FES Scale | MZA | MZT | DZA | DZT | Model-Fitting Heritability |
|---|---|---|---|---|---|
| *Primary* | | | | | |
| Cohesion | .41 | .60 | .32 | .43 | .22 |
| Expressiveness | .22 | .45 | .07 | .25 | .24* |
| Conflict | .35 | .58 | .18 | .46 | .32* |
| Achievement | .39 | .45 | .16 | .31 | .35* |
| Cultural | .33 | .61 | .22 | .43 | .31* |
| Active | .38 | .60 | .28 | .47 | .25* |
| Organization | .12 | .53 | .17 | .32 | .24* |
| Control | −.03 | .52 | .21 | .29 | .15 |
| *Second-Order* | | | | | |
| Relationship (warmth) | .37 | .66 | .29 | .42 | .38* |
| System Maintenance (control) | .00 | .60 | .17 | .31 | .11 |
| Personal Growth | .42 | .53 | .26 | .45 | .19* |

SOURCE: Plomin, R., McClearn, G. E., Pedersen, N. L., Nesselroade, J. R., & Bergeman, C. S. (1988). Genetic influence on childhood family environment perceived retrospectively from the last half of the life span. *Developmental Psychology, 24,* 738-745. Copyright 1988 by the American Psychological Association. Reprinted by permission of the publisher.
NOTE: Sample sizes varied from 74-84 pairs for MZA, 128-135 for MZT, 185-192 for DZA, and 171-181 for DZT.
* Significant (*p* < .05) model-fitting test of heritability comparing reduced models.

and Conflict primary scales. Another second-order dimension called Personal Growth involves the remaining primary scales of Achievement, Cultural, and Active primary scales. The Personal Growth dimension also yields significant heritability ($h^2$ = .19).

The SATSA results were confirmed in a small study of reared-apart twins (45 MZA and 26 DZA pairs) from 19 to 68 years of age (Bouchard & McGue, 1990). The heritability estimate for the warmth factor was .31 and for the control factor it was .15. The individual FES scales also confirmed the SATSA results: Heritabilities for the cohesion and conflict scales were .31 and .30, respectively, whereas for the control scale heritability was only .10. Another twin study of adults' retrospective reports of the family in which they were reared found results for twins reared together that further confirm these findings and are quite similar to the results of Rowe's (1983) original study (Jang, 1993). For cohesion and conflict, model-fitting heritability estimates are .58 and .61, respectively, and for control the heritability estimate is .00 in a study of 89 MZT, 49 same-sex DZT, and 65 same-sex non-twin sibling pairs from 16 to 45 years of age.

In SATSA, twins reared together are more similar than twins reared apart for all scales. This is not surprising because, as in Rowe's studies, the twins reared together rate the same family. What is surprising is that correlations for twins reared apart are generally significant even though the co-twins are reporting on different families. Moreover, just as MZT correlations exceed DZT correlations, MZA correlations exceed DZA correlations for all but the two control-related scales of Organization and Control. Finding genetic effects using this adoption design adds substantially to confidence in the results of classical twin studies that compare MZT and DZT. But the real surprise in these adoption results needs emphasis. The MZA and DZA co-twins are reporting on *different* families. If the MZA and DZA correlations had been zero, we would have just shrugged them off saying, "Of course, what else would you expect given that the co-twins are rating different families?"

How can genetic effects emerge when the co-twins are rating different families? There are at least three possibilities. First, similarities in the family environments of reared-apart twins could be due to selective placement in that the families in which the two twins were reared might in fact be similar. This seems unlikely because selective placement in SATSA appears to be modest (Pedersen, McClearn, Plomin, & Nesselroade, 1992). Moreover, selective placement could account for the genetic evidence only with the additional awkward assumption that adopted-apart MZ twins were placed in more similar family environments than adopted-apart DZ twins. Half the twins were separated before their first birthday when it is difficult to know whether twins are identical or fraternal.

A second interpretation involves the subjective, self-report nature of the FES. Finding heritability for twins reared apart in different families could be due to genetic effects on general attributional processes that affect perceptions of the environment.

That is, genetic effects could be in the eye of the beholder—for example, wearing genetically fashioned rose-colored or dark-tinted glasses that color the family environment through the blur of half a century.

The third interpretation is the most interesting in relation to the hyphen in nature-nurture. It is possible that subjective reports on the FES are veridical. If the twins' perceptions are veridical, the most likely explanation for finding genetic effects in the data for reared-apart twins is that members of the two families responded similarly to genetically influenced characteristics of the separated twins or that the twins contributed to similar family dynamics. Although it is tempting to interpret these findings further at this point, an extended discussion is better placed after all the relevant research is described.

In summary, genetics has been implicated not only in Rowe's two twin studies that employed measures of adolescents' perceptions of their family environment but also in SATSA, which employed perceptions of middle-aged adults of their rearing family environment half a century earlier. SATSA combined the adoption design with the classical twin design. These adoption data yielded the intriguing finding that MZA are more similar than DZA in reporting on their family environments even though both types of twins were reared in different families. The SATSA results extend Rowe's findings by suggesting that genetic factors contribute not only to warmth but to several facets of family environment, other than those indexing control.

## REPORTS OF RELATIVE DIFFERENCES IN FAMILY ENVIRONMENTS

Three sibling studies used a different type of questionnaire concerning the family environment. The Sibling Inventory of Differential Experience (SIDE) was developed to assess nonshared (differential) experiences of siblings, not just in relation to parents but also to each other and to peers (Daniels & Plomin, 1985). The novel aspect of the SIDE is that it asks siblings to rate their experiences relative to their siblings rather than in an absolute sense. For example, one of the SIDE differential parental treatment items is, "Mother has been sensitive to what we think and feel." Each sibling answers on a 5-point scale in which 1 represents "toward sibling much more," 3 means "same toward my sibling and me," and 5 means "toward me much more." The motivation behind the construction of the SIDE was that children should be able to rate relative differences in their experiences as compared to their sibling more easily than they can make absolute judgments. The usual strategy of questionnaires involves such absolute judgments. For example, the question about maternal sensitivity would typically be asked in the following manner: How sensitive is your mother to what you think and feel? The child might be asked to respond on a 5-point scale in which 1 signifies "rarely" and 5 indicates "nearly all of the time."

This novel approach of relative ratings seems particularly well suited to research on nonshared environment, which was the purpose for which the SIDE was designed. However, the relative ratings present a challenge for genetic analysis. Why not just compute sibling correlations as is usually done for questionnaires? An approach like this has been taken in one twin study using the SIDE (Jang, 1993). The problem is that such sibling correlations do not involve only the similarity of their treatment. They also involve the degree of sibling agreement about differential treatment, an interesting topic but not the issue at hand. For example, siblings might not agree at all about whom their mother loved best because in some pairs both siblings say that mother loved them best and in other pairs both siblings say their mother loved the other one best. John Loehlin (personal communication, January 31, 1993) has pointed out that MZ twins might agree more than DZ twins but have smaller differences to judge than DZ twins. These two processes may offset each other and lead to similar correlations for MZ and DZ twins.

The SIDE difference scores themselves express how similarly or differently the siblings perceive themselves to be treated, independent of the siblings' agreement about differential treatment. However, these relative difference scores cannot just be averaged because the average difference should be near the midpoint rating of 3 for both MZ and DZ twins. One way around this problem with ratings of relative sibling differences for genetic analyses is to transform the relative differences to absolute (unsigned) differences. Absolute differences indicate perceived differences in experience regardless of which twin reported more of a particular experience. The transformation is accomplished by changing a 3 (no difference) to 0, changing scores of 2 or 4 (slight difference) to 1, and changing scores of 1 or 5 (much difference) to 2. For example, regardless of whether an individual felt that mother was much more affectionate to the sibling or much more affectionate to the individual, that individual's relative score of 1 ("toward sibling much more") or 5 ("toward me much more") would be transformed to an absolute difference score of 2 (much difference). The relative difference scores of each individual are transformed in this way to an absolute difference score. Because the absolute difference is calculated from each individual's relative difference score, the absolute difference scores do not assess sibling agreement.

As in the case of relative difference scores, we cannot simply calculate sibling correlations because such correlations address the issue of sibling agreement about differences, not the differences themselves. Instead, average absolute differences can be compared for different groups of siblings. For example, if the average absolute difference is smaller for MZ than DZ twins, genetic effects are implicated. Although we can test for the significance of such differences and estimate effect size in relation to such difference scores, an unsolved problem is the calculation of a meaningful heritability estimate from such difference scores. The SIDE was used in a twin study (Baker & Daniels, 1990), in an adoption study (Daniels & Plomin, 1985), and in the Nonshared Environment in Adolescent Development project (NEAD), which includes twins as well as other sibling relationships (Pike, Manke, Hetherington, Reiss, & Plomin, 1993). The twin study (Baker & Daniels, 1990) included 235 pairs of adult twins who responded retrospectively about the family in which they were reared. Table 2.3 lists absolute sibling differences (and standard deviations of these differences) for the eight scales of the SIDE that involve family environment. (The peer scales are discussed in the next

**TABLE 2.3** MZ and DZ Within-Pair Sibling Differences on the SIDE in Adult Twins

| SIDE Scales | MZ diff (SD) | | DZ diff (SD) |
|---|---|---|---|
| Maternal Affection | .27 (.35) | * | .41 (.44) |
| Paternal Affection | .26 (.38) | * | .50 (.51) |
| Maternal Control | .21 (.40) | * | .40 (.52) |
| Paternal Control | .19 (.39) | * | .46 (.60) |
| Sibling Closeness | .51 (.51) | * | .74 (.52) |
| Sibling Antagonism | .61 (.45) | | .76 (.42) |
| Sibling Caretaking | .66 (.43) | | .76 (.41) |
| Sibling Jealousy | .62 (.45) | * | .81 (.45) |

SOURCE: Adapted from Baker & Daniels (1990). A similar version of this table appeared in Plomin, R., & Bergeman, C. S. (1991). The nature of nuture: Genetic influence on "environmental" measures. *Behavior and Brain Sciences, 14,* 373-427. Reprinted with permission of Cambridge University Press.
NOTE: Sample includes 139-161 MZ pairs and 61-74 DZ pairs.
* Mean of MZ difference significantly ($p < .05$) lower than mean of DZ.

chapter, which focuses on extrafamilial influences.) DZ differences are greater than MZ differences for all eight SIDE scales and the differences are significant for six of the eight scales. Unlike the results of Rowe's studies and SATSA, significant genetic effects are found for perceptions of mothers' and fathers' control as well as affection. This may be due to the use of differential rather than absolute ratings. A new finding is that genetics is implicated for some aspects of the sibling environment as well as the parenting environment. DZ differences are significantly greater than MZ differences for the warmth scale of sibling closeness and for sibling jealousy, but not for sibling caretaking or sibling antagonism.

Table 2.4 presents results for adolescent twins in NEAD (Pike et al., 1993). The results are similar for the two co-twins in each pair. Two differences stand out for these adolescent twins in this report as compared to the adult twins in the report by Baker and Daniels (Table 2.3). First, adolescent twins, both MZ and DZ, rate their parental and sibling treatment as less differential than the adult twins. This difference may be influenced by the use of retrospective reports of family life by the adult twins, implying that as time goes by perceptions of differences are exaggerated. However, the

**TABLE 2.4**  MZ and DZ Within-Pair Differences on the SIDE in Adolescent Twins

| | Twin 1 | | Twin 2 | |
| --- | --- | --- | --- | --- |
| SIDE Scales | MZ diff (SD) | DZ diff (SD) | MZ diff (SD) | DZ diff (SD) |
| Maternal Affection | .13 (.29) | .20 (.28) | .14 (.24) | .16 (.26) |
| Paternal Affection | .09 (.19) | .16 (.32) | .09 (.18) | .12 (.23) |
| Maternal Control | .20 (.34) | .31 (.40) | .22 (.36) | .33 (.42) |
| Paternal Control | .09 (.21) | .19 (.39) | .13 (.26) | .21 (.29) |
| Sibling Closeness | .33 (.45) | .44 (.46) | .33 (.41) | .43 (.40) |
| Sibling Antagonism | .44 (.38) * | .55 (.41) | .44 (.37) * | .58 (.35) |
| Sibling Caretaking | .50 (.40) | .61 (.44) | .45 (.33) * | .64 (.39) |
| Sibling Jealousy | .39 (.40) * | .50 (.40) | .34 (.34) * | .50 (.38) |

SOURCE: Adapted from Pike, Manke, Hetherington, Reiss, & Plomin (1993).
NOTE: Sample includes 93 MZ pairs and 98 DZ pairs.
* Mean of MZ difference significantly ($p < .05$) lower than mean of DZ.

FES does not show this pattern of results when Rowe's results for adolescent twins (Table 2.1) are compared to the retrospective results from SATSA (Table 2.2), although it is possible that the relative ratings of the SIDE are more sensitive to such effects.

The second difference between Tables 2.3 and 2.4 involves the pattern of genetic effects. Although some genetic effects are suggested for the SIDE parent scales, with the exception of parental affection, significant genetic effects for the adolescent twins emerge for the sibling scales rather than the parent scales (Table 2.4). In contrast, the results for the adult twins show significant genetic effects to a greater extent for the parent scales than the sibling scales (Table 2.3).

An ongoing 3-year follow-up of the NEAD sample will be useful in testing the hypothesis that these differences are due to age rather than to alternative explanations such as chance differences between samples or the use of a retrospective version of the SIDE in the adult sample. It should also be mentioned that the NEAD project included 95 pairs of full siblings in nondivorced families.

The results for these siblings were very similar to the DZ results, suggesting that twins' ratings of their treatment by parents and siblings are not more similar than ratings by non-twin siblings. One adoption study supports the interpretation that, for adolescents, SIDE sibling differential treatment shows greater genetic effects than parental differential treatment (Daniels & Plomin, 1985). This study employed the sibling adoption design that compares nonadoptive siblings (biological siblings in nonadoptive families) and adoptive siblings (pairs of genetically unrelated children adopted early in life into the same family). The study included 384 adolescent and young adult pairs. Results are shown in Table 2.5. Although these results suggest less genetic influence than the twin results, genetic effects are suggested for the sibling scales rather than the parenting scales, a result similar to the adolescent twin results shown in Table 2.4.

However, another study yields different results, which may be due to the use of a different design (Pike et al., 1993). In addition to MZ and DZ twins and full siblings in nondivorced families mentioned earlier, NEAD included 182 pairs of full siblings in stepfamilies and 130 pairs of unrelated siblings in stepfamilies. The SIDE results for this quasi-adoption design are shown in Table 2.6. Significant genetic effects emerge for the parent scales rather than the sibling scales. Caution is warranted, however, because perceptions of differential treatment seem likely to be affected in stepfamilies, especially for unrelated siblings in which both the remarried mother and father bring a child from a former marriage.

In summary, the relative ratings of the SIDE are quite different from traditional measures and present problems for genetic analysis. Nonetheless, some evidence for genetic effects emerges from these twin and adoption studies, although more research is needed to clarify differences between studies. Future research using the SIDE might also follow up on the hypothesis that genetic effects for adolescents are found primarily for sibling treatment rather than parent treatment and vice versa for adults.

**TABLE 2.5**    Nonadoptive and Adoptive Within-Pair Differences on the SIDE in Adolescents and Young Adults

| SIDE Scales | Nonadoptive diff (SD) | | Adoptive diff (SD) |
|---|---|---|---|
| Maternal Affection | .49 (.45) | | .49 (.44) |
| Paternal Affection | .54 (.48) | | .50 (.45) |
| Maternal Control | .64 (.51) | | .62 (.48) |
| Paternal Control | .69 (.54) | | .64 (.50) |
| Sibling Closeness | .62 (.46) | * | .78 (.46) |
| Sibling Antagonism | .75 (.38) | | .83 (.37) |
| Sibling Caretaking | .79 (.32) | | .85 (.35) |
| Sibling Jealousy | .83 (.45) | | .89 (.43) |

SOURCE: Adapted from Daniels & Plomin (1985). A similar version of this table appeared in Plomin, R., & Bergeman, C. S. (1991). The nature of nurture: Genetic influence on "environmental" measures. *Behavior and Brain Sciences, 14,* 373-427. Reprinted with permission of Cambridge University Press.
NOTE: Sample includes 149-179 pairs of nonadoptive siblings and 185-205 pairs of adoptive siblings.
* Mean of nonadoptive siblings significantly lower than mean of adoptive siblings.

A SYSTEMATIC EXAMINATION
OF FAMILY ENVIRONMENT MEASURES

Other than the NEAD project, the genetic studies previously described were not designed specifically to investigate genetic contributions to environmental measures. They were focused on other issues such as personality and happened to include one or two environmental measures. In contrast, the NEAD project was the first study to focus on the systematic examination of diverse measures of the family environment in the context of a genetic design. Measures included 72 scales that assessed relationships, expression of affection, discipline, monitoring, disagreements, and conflict tactics.

Of the 72 scales, 54 showed significant genetic effects in model-fitting analyses, and the average heritability estimate for the 72 measures was .26, suggesting that about a quarter of the variance of these environmental measures can be accounted for by genetic differences among children (Plomin, Reiss, Hetherington, & Howe, in press). As in the previous studies, measures of both parental behavior and sibling behavior showed genetic effects.

TABLE 2.6  Within-Pair Differences for Adolescent Full Siblings and Un-related Siblings in Stepfamilies on the SIDE

| SIDE Scales | Older Child | | Younger Child | |
| | Full Sib diff (SD) | Un. Sib diff (SD) | Full Sib diff (SD) | Un. Sib diff (SD) |
|---|---|---|---|---|
| Maternal Affection | .30 (.38) * | .47 (.49) | .28 (.39) * | .46 (.51) |
| Paternal Affection | .23 (.37) * | .41 (.53) | .24 (.37) * | .35 (.48) |
| Maternal Control | .43 (.43) | .49 (.47) | .40 (.44) * | .52 (.51) |
| Paternal Control | .29 (.38) * | .39 (.50) | .29 (.40) | .36 (.49) |
| Sibling Closeness | .44 (.44) | .40 (.41) | .49 (.49) | .41 (.45) |
| Sibling Antagonism | .57 (.36) | .54 (.39) | .62 (.43) | .49 (.38) |
| Sibling Caretaking | .69 (.39) | .64 (.45) | .70 (.45) | .59 (.43) |
| Sibling Jealousy | .55 (.38) | .43 (.41) | .58 (.43) | .50 (.41) |

SOURCE: Adapted from Pike, Manke, Hetherington, Reiss, & Plomin (1993).
NOTE: Sample includes 182 pairs of full siblings and 130 pairs of unrelated siblings, all in stepfamilies.
* Mean of full siblings significantly lower than mean of unrelated siblings.

For example, adolescent ratings of their closeness to their mother yielded correlations of .53 for MZ, .37 for DZ, and .28 for full siblings in nondivorced families. These results suggest a genetic contribution and possibly some greater similarity for DZ twins than for full siblings. The novel aspect of the design involved stepfamilies with full siblings, half siblings, and unrelated siblings. The sibling correlations for these three groups for the maternal closeness measure are not pretty: .04, .20, and −.10, respectively. The comparison between the correlation of .28 for full siblings in non-divorced families and .04 for full siblings in stepfamilies suggests the possibility of decreased resemblance in stepfamilies. Although the half-sibling correlation is relatively high, the correlation for unrelated siblings is the lowest of the six correlations. Model-fitting is particularly useful in such multiple-group comparisons in order to analyze all of the data simultaneously. For the scale of maternal closeness, the model-fitting estimate of heritability is significant and substantial ($h^2$ = .51).

In contrast to this warmth-related scale, the most direct measure of control yielded the lowest estimate of heritability ($h^2$ = .10 for mothers and .18 for fathers). Significant heritability was found for adolescents' ratings of both mothers and fathers for several dimensions not included in previous research, such as punitiveness, reasoning during conflict, and monitoring.

Because the results of this study are so voluminous, they are summarized in Table 2.7 in relation to composite measures of positive, negative, and monitoring behavior derived from factor analyses of the 72 measures. The table includes model-fitting estimates of variance components by target (parent or sibling) and by respondent (child or parent). The first eight rows report results for the adolescents' ratings of their parents and their siblings. The average heritability estimate is .33 for ratings of mother and .42 for ratings of father. For the shared environment parameter, the average estimates are .15 for mothers and .10 for fathers. Most of the variance is due to nonshared environment plus error of measurement. Adolescents' ratings of their siblings also show genetic effects ($h^2 = .33$ on average). The rest of Table 2.7, which suggests that heritability does not depend on respondent, is discussed in the following section.

In summary, this first systematic study of diverse measures of family environment confirms the results of earlier studies in suggesting a genetic contribution to children's perceptions of many facets of their family environment.

## Research on Parents' Perceptions of Family Environment

The research reviewed up until this point involved children's ratings of their parents and siblings. Are genetic effects limited to children's perceptions of the family environment? One extension of this research is the investigation of parents' perceptions. Two types of genetic designs have been used. In a twin study, the twins can be the target children who rate their parents' treatment, as in the research discussed until now. Parents can also rate their own behavior toward each of the twins. This design in which the twins are the children can be called a child-based genetic design. In the

**TABLE 2.7** NEAD Components of Variance by Respondent and Target

| Respondent | Target | Composite | $e_n^2$ | $e_s^2$ | $h^2$ |
|---|---|---|---|---|---|
| Child | Mother | Positive | .50 | .20* | .30* |
| | | Negative | .46 | .14* | .40* |
| | | Monitoring | .61 | .10* | .29* |
| Child | Father | Positive | .38 | .06 | .56* |
| | | Negative | .53 | .24* | .23 |
| | | Monitoring | .53 | .01 | .46* |
| Child | Sibling | Positive | .27 | .37* | .36* |
| | | Negative | .30 | .41* | .29* |
| Mother | Mother | Positive | .10 | .52* | .38* |
| | | Negative | .08 | .38* | .53* |
| | | Monitoring | .01 | .98* | .03 |
| Father | Father | Positive | .07 | .71* | .22* |
| | | Negative | .10 | .61* | .30* |
| | | Monitoring | .02 | .98* | .02 |
| Mother | Sibling | Positive | .08 | .71* | .21* |
| | | Negative | .11 | .71* | .19* |
| Father | Sibling | Positive | .08 | .83* | .11* |
| | | Negative | .10 | .81* | .10* |

SOURCE: Adapted from Plomin, Reiss, Hetherington, & Howe (in press).
NOTE: Model-fitting estimates of nonshared environment/error ($e_n^2$), shared environment ($e_s^2$), and heritability ($h^2$). Significance of $e_s^2$ and $h^2$ was based on chi-square change from the standard model to a reduced model in which these parameters were separately set to zero. Estimates are based on a best-fitting model—either the standard model or models that allowed different $e_s^2$ for siblings (1) in nondivorced versus stepfamilies or (2) in twins versus non-twin siblings.
* $p < .05$.

child-based genetic design, the distinction between child ratings and parent ratings is more than methodological. Genetic effects could emerge for twin and adoptee children's perceptions of their family environment for many more reasons than is the case for their parents' perceptions. For children's ratings, genetic effects could occur as a result of any cognitive or personality factors that affect their perceptions of parental treatment. In contrast, for the parents' ratings, a genetic contribution will be seen only to the extent that the parents' perceptions of their behavior to their children depends on genetic factors of the children, not on genetic factors of the parents themselves. Subjective processes entailed in the parents' ratings do not contribute to genetic effects in analyses of child-based genetic designs. This would lead to greater heritability for child-based genetic designs to the extent that such subjective processes are involved in ratings by children and parents. A second design becomes possible when parental reports are employed: The parents themselves can be the twins. This can be called a parent-based genetic design. In contrast to the child-based genetic design, when parents rate their parenting behavior in a parent-based genetic design, any genetically influenced characteristics of the parents that affect their perceptions of parenting will contribute to heritability of parenting.

CHILD-BASED GENETIC DESIGNS

Three studies using child-based genetic designs are discussed in this section.

*NEAD.* In addition to children's ratings, the NEAD project described in the previous section also included parents' ratings of their treatment toward each of their adolescent children and of the adolescent siblings' treatment of each other. When parents rate their behavior toward each of the two siblings, sibling correlations are about twice as great as when the two siblings rate their parent, probably because a single person is rating both children. This results in the much greater estimates of shared environmental influence shown in the second half of Table 2.7. In the case of the monitoring composite, parents report that they treat their children the same. That is, nearly all of the variance is attributed to shared environment because the sibling correlations are extremely high for all four groups. (As indicated in the top of the Table 2.7, children report that they are treated differently by their parents, even for the monitoring composite.)

However, the genetic message from these results is that the pattern of sibling correlations yields significant heritabilities for parents' ratings of their own positive and negative behavior and the siblings' behavior. This is an important finding because it suggests that genetic effects are not only in the heads of the twins or adoptees who rate their parents. As noted earlier, in a child-based genetic design, parental ratings will show genetic effects only if they reflect genetically influenced characteristics of the children, not of the parents. As expected on the basis of this reasoning, heritabilities are somewhat lower for parental reports than for child reports.

Another interesting aspect of the results is the support they provide for the hypothesis that parental control shows less heritability than other dimensions of parenting. Although the positive and negative composites yielded significant heritability, heritability estimates were negligible for the monitoring composite. In the case of parental reports, however, negligible heritability occurs because parents report that they do not differentiate their two children on this dimension of parenting.

*Colorado Adoption Project.* The Colorado Adoption Project also included parental reports of parenting when their children were 7 and again at 9 years of age. A measure of parenting style (Dibble & Cohen, 1974) was used that assesses eight socially desirable and eight socially undesirable parenting techniques and yields three factors: warmth, control, and inconsistent parenting. The results for the three factors for the sibling adoption design are presented in Table 2.8 (Braungart, in press). At both 7 and 9 years, the warmth scale is heritable and the control scale is not significantly heritable. The high heritabilities for the warmth factor are surprising in light of the issues discussed earlier concerning parent ratings in a child-based genetic design. In this first report of parental inconsistency, the results are themselves inconsistent, suggesting heritability at 9 years but not 7 years.

*Goodman and Stevenson.* A study of 200 pairs of 13-year-old twins involved a lengthy interview with parents in which parental warmth and criticism by both mothers and fathers were assessed toward each twin separately (Goodman & Stevenson, 1991). Table 2.9 lists the percentages of twin pairs who experienced the same degree of parental warmth or criticism. These parental interviews suggest genetic effects in that parental warmth and criticism are more

**TABLE 2.8**  Nonadoptive and Adoptive Sibling Correlations and Model-Fitting Heritabilities for Parental Reports on a Measure of Parenting Style When the Children Were 7 and 9 Years Old

| Factor | 7 Years | | | 9 Years | | |
|---|---|---|---|---|---|---|
| | Nonadoptive | Adoptive | $h^2$ | Nonadoptive | Adoptive | $h^2$ |
| Warmth | .76 | .42 | .56* | .79 | .52 | .40* |
| Control | .74 | .63 | .18 | .48 | .56 | .00 |
| Inconsistency | .56 | .68 | .00 | .57 | .33 | .46* |

SOURCE: Adapted from Braungart (in press).
NOTE: N at 7 years = 49-51 nonadoptive pairs and 46-49 adoptive pairs. N at 9 years = 43-46 and 31-33, respectively.
* $p < .05$.

similar for MZ than for DZ twins. A novel feature of this study was an analysis comparing MZ twins who were correctly recognized as MZ twins by their parents and MZ twins who were mistakenly labeled as DZ twins by their parents. The results are very similar for the two groups of twins, suggesting that the results depend on true zygosity rather than on parental beliefs about zygosity. In other words, these results support the reasonableness of the equal environments assumption (see earlier discussion) specifically in relation to a measure of parenting.

It should be emphasized that the genetic designs of these three studies hinge on the children rather than the parents. That is, the children, not the parents, are twins and adoptees. The following section considers genetic designs in which the parents are the twins and adoptees.

PARENT-BASED GENETIC DESIGNS

In contrast to genetic designs that are based on children as twins and adoptees, it is possible to use parent-based genetic designs. For example, adult twins who are parents can be asked to report on their own parenting. As discussed in the previous section, child-based genetic designs are able to detect genetically influenced subjective processes that affect the children's ratings of their parents but not genetically influenced subjective processes in-

**TABLE 2.9** Percentages of Twin Pairs Experiencing the Same Degree of
Parental Warmth or Criticism

| | Percentage of Concordant Twin Pairs | | |
| --- | --- | --- | --- |
| Scale | Recognized MZ | Unrecognized MZ | Same-Sex DZ |
| Maternal warmth | 85% (59/69) | 83% (20/24) | 71% (77/109) |
| Paternal warmth | 94% (50/53) | 82% (14/17) | 64% (51/80) |
| Maternal criticism | 86% (59/69) | 92% (22/24) | 57% (61/108) |
| Paternal criticism | 76% (40/53) | 77% (13/17) | 70% (55/79) |

SOURCE: Plomin, R., & Bergeman, C. S. (1991a). The nature of nurture: Genetic influence on
"environmental" measures. *Behavior and Brain Sciences, 14,* 373-427 (with Open Peer Commentary). Reprinted with permission of Cambridge University Press.

volved in their parents' ratings. Parent-based genetic designs are
complementary in that they can detect genetic effects on the subjective processes that might affect the parents' ratings of their
behavior toward their children.

In SATSA, an abbreviated version of the Family Environment
Scales (FES) was completed by 179 reared-apart twin pairs and 207
reared-together pairs in relation to each twins' current family, that
is, the family consisting of the adult twin subject and his or her
spouse and children (Plomin, McClearn, Pedersen, Nesselroade,
& Bergeman, 1989). It should be noted that parenting per se was
not assessed but rather perceptions of the general family environment. To the extent that the FES assesses not only characteristics
of the parents but also characteristics of the spouse and children,
it could dilute estimates of genetic effects when parents are the
target of the genetic analysis.

Results of this study are summarized in Table 2.10. The average
MZA correlation is .25, ranging from .10 for Cohesion to .45 for
Culture. Because the MZA correlation directly estimates heritability, this suggests that about a quarter of the variance of the FES
scales can be attributed to genetic factors. The average model-fitting heritability estimate based on all of the data is similar (24%),
with the lowest estimate for Achievement (12%) and the highest
estimate for Culture (40%). Heritability estimates were statistically significant ($p < .05$) for Expressiveness, Culture, Organization, and Control, and marginally significant ($p < .10$) for Conflict

**TABLE 2.10** SATSA Twin Correlations and Heritabilities for Adult Twins'
Ratings of Their Current Family Environment

| FES Scale | Twin Correlations | | | | Model-Fitting Heritability |
|---|---|---|---|---|---|
|  | MZA | MZT | DZA | DZT |  |
| Cohesion | .10 | .30 | −.11 | −.09 | .19 |
| Expressiveness | .37 | .22 | .01 | .11 | .27* |
| Conflict | .16 | .27 | .13 | .06 | .25 |
| Achievement | .16 | .23 | .05 | .19 | .12 |
| Culture | .45 | .37 | .26 | .10 | .40* |
| Active | .12 | .37 | .08 | .07 | .21 |
| Organization | .30 | .31 | .13 | .13 | .26* |
| Control | .36 | .18 | .21 | .12 | .26* |

SOURCE: Adapted from Plomin, McClearn, Pedersen, Nesselroade, & Bergeman (1989).
NOTE: Samples sizes varied from 40-50 pairs for MZA, 82-92 for MZT, 120-129 for DZA, and
104-115 for DZT.
* Significant ($p < .05$) model-fitting test of heritability comparing reduced models.

and Active. For every scale, the classical twin design yielded MZT
correlations that exceeded DZT correlations and the adoption
design yielded MZA correlations that exceeded DZA correlations.

It is interesting that, unlike the child-based genetic designs, this
parent-based design yielded significant genetic heritability for
control. One possibility is that this difference is a result of using a
parent-based rather than child-based genetic design. In this study,
twin parents reported on their own parenting, whereas in the
previous studies, twin children rated the parenting of their mothers and fathers. Genetically influenced characteristics of parents
may contribute to their perceptions of their own control (parent-
based design), even though the same measures may not reflect
genetically influenced characteristics of the children (child-based
design). One reasonable hypothesis is that this finding is due to
parents' greater contribution to control in the family as compared
to the control wielded by children. Loehlin (personal communication, January 31, 1993) has suggested another possibility. Twins-
as-children are in the same family, and there are presumably
strong social pressures toward equal standards in the application
of discipline to them. Twins-as-adults rearing their own children

are involved in two different families, and such constraints on equal treatment between families are much weaker.

Preliminary reports of two other genetic studies using parent-based designs confirm these findings. One study involved adult MZ and DZ twins and adult adoptive siblings all of whom currently had their own families with children under 10 years of age (Rowe, Callor, Harmon-Losoya, & Goldsmith, 1992). Model-fitting analyses of data from the three groups indicated significant heritability for a control factor as well as for a warmth factor. Another study of more than a thousand pairs of parent twins also found significant heritability for both control and warmth factors and suggested greater heritability for mothers than for fathers (Perusse, Neale, Heath, & Eaves, 1992).

## A PARENT-OFFSPRING ADOPTION STUDY IN MIDDLE CHILDHOOD

A recent report from the Colorado Adoption Project bridges child-based and parent-based genetic designs. The study represents a parent-offspring adoption study that investigates resemblance between parental perceptions and child perceptions of family environment (Chipuer, Merriwether-Devries, & Plomin, 1993). The parent-offspring adoption design compares resemblance between adoptive parents and their adopted children with resemblance between nonadoptive parents and their offspring. Genetic effects are inferred when parent-offspring correlations are greater in nonadoptive families than in adoptive families. A second novel aspect of this study was its attempt to assess perceptions of much younger children than previous studies. A 20-question card sort version of five dimensions of the FES was constructed for interviewer-guided administration to 7-year-old children.

Resemblance between maternal reports on the FES and the reports of their children at 7 years of age was compared for 183 adoptive families and 162 nonadoptive families and for paternal reports in about half of the families. Despite the differences in measures and in age for the parents and children, modest parent-offspring resemblance emerged that tended to be greater in

**TABLE 2.11** Parent-Offspring Correlations for Nonadoptive and Adoptive Parents and Their 7-Year-Old Children

|  | Mother | | Father | |
|  | Nonadoptive | Adoptive | Nonadoptive | Adoptive |
|---|---|---|---|---|
| Cohesion | .35 | −.08 | .24 | .02 |
| Conflict | .18 | .07 | −.01 | .06 |
| Control | .23 | .02 | .10 | .09 |
| Expressive | .09 | −.04 | .18 | .06 |
| Achievement | .05 | .25 | .35 | .19 |

SOURCE: Adapted from Chipuer, Merriwether-Devries, & Plomin (1993).
NOTE: The number of mother-child pairs is 154 in nonadoptive families and 176 in adoptive families; the number of father-child pairs is 85 and 88, respectively.

nonadoptive than in adoptive families, as shown in Table 2.11. Genetic effects are implicated for the major warmth dimension of cohesion for both mothers and fathers. The other scales suggested genetic effects for either the mothers or the fathers, although not for both. These results indicate that views of the family environment shared by parents and their offspring (not just by siblings as in previous research) may show a genetic contribution even when the offspring are as young as 7 years. It should be noted that a sibling adoption analysis of these data yielded significant heritabilities for conflict and achievement but not for the other scales (Braungart, in press).

WHY NO GENETIC CONTRIBUTION
FOR PARENTAL CONTROL?

Although I have tried to focus on data rather than interpretation in order to document the phenomenon of genetic effects on environmental measures, this is an appropriate place to mention an interesting hypothesis concerning parental control. Why does parental control show less heritability than other parenting dimensions in child-based genetic designs? Why does parental control appear to show heritability in parent-based designs? Lytton (1991) suggested that, for parental warmth, influence runs mainly from the child to the parent. In contrast, the control-compliance literature suggests that parental control runs much more from parent to child (Lytton, 1980). In his own words:

> [for parental warmth] the child is the dominant force, because parents do not set out on a purposeful program to create or direct attachment to them, and acceptance is also largely a matter of the child's disposition and relationship with the parent, rather than the parent's conscious choice. On the other hand, most parents do engage in a conscious, purpose-driven program of shaping and controlling the child's behavior—hence it is their dispositions that count here. (Lytton, 1991, p. 399)

As indicated in the next section on observational measures of the family environment, the finding of less heritability for parental control than other dimensions of parenting is less clear than it is for self-report data. Nonetheless, even if Lytton's hypothesis were limited to self-report data, the hypothesis may be heuristically useful for exploring the etiology of individual differences in perceptions of the family environment.

## Observational Research on the Family Environment

The previously discussed body of research depended entirely on questionnaires. The most obvious direction for research was to investigate whether genetic effects are limited to perceptions. In this section, four observational studies are reviewed.

### HOME OBSERVATION FOR MEASUREMENT OF THE ENVIRONMENT IN CAP

One of the most widely used measures of the home environment in relation to cognitive development in infancy is an observational/interview measure called the Home Observation for Measurement of the Environment (HOME; Caldwell & Bradley, 1978). For example, the first of the 45 HOME items is "mother spontaneously vocalizes to child at least twice during visit." The HOME was designed to predict children's cognitive development using proximal measures of the home environment that go beyond socioeconomic status.

A sibling adoption study has been reported for the total HOME score for nearly 200 pairs of nonadoptive and adoptive siblings in which each sibling's home environment was assessed when the child was 12 and 24 months of age as part of the longitudinal Colorado Adoption Project (Braungart, Fulker, Plomin, & DeFries, 1992). As shown in Table 2.12, the adoptive sibling correlations indicate the presence of shared environmental influence, which is to be expected given that the HOME assesses the "same" home for both children even though the HOME is administered with a time lag from 1 to 3 years apart for the two children in each family.

More to the present point, at both ages, nonadoptive sibling correlations are greater than those for adoptive siblings, suggesting genetic contributions to the HOME. Model-fitting analyses confirmed significant heritability for the HOME and estimated that about 40% of the variance of the HOME is genetic in origin. Although a HOME-like measure constructed for the CAP for use at 3 and 4 years showed little heritability (Braungart, in press), the measure is problematic in several ways, such as its low reliability and low correlation with IQ (Plomin, DeFries, & Fulker, 1988). Nonetheless, this finding may represent a true developmental trend. For example, parental responsiveness in infancy may be more susceptible to genetically influenced characteristics of infants than in childhood when situational factors may play a larger role in parental behavior.

Analyses of HOME items suggest different developmental patterns. For example, items related to maternal warmth (e.g., mother praises child, mother's voice is positive, mother caresses and kisses child) show genetic effects at 12 months but not at 24 months (Saudino, 1993). In contrast, several items concerning toys (e.g., eye-hand combinatorial toys, toys for literature and music, "maturing" toys) suggest genetic effects at 24 months but not at 12 months. A similar developmental trend appears for an item, "number of physical punishments last week." This item showed no heritability at 12 months, slight heritability at 2 years, and

**TABLE 2.12** Correlations for Nonadoptive and Adoptive Siblings and Model-Fitting Results for the HOME Total Score at Ages 1 and 2

|  | Sibling Correlations | | Model-Fitting |
|  | Nonadoptive | Adoptive | Heritability |
| --- | --- | --- | --- |
| 1 year | .58* | .35* | .41* |
| 2 years | .57* | .40* | .40* |

SOURCE: Adapted from Braungart, Fulker, Plomin, & DeFries (1992).
NOTE: Sample sizes for nonadoptive and adoptive sibling pairs were 105 and 87, respectively, at 1 year and 103 and 86 at 2 years.
* Significant ($p < .05$).

substantial heritability at 3 and 4 years. Analyses of the traditional HOME scales suggest that the scales of Maternal Involvement and Variety of Daily Stimulation are primarily responsible for genetic effects on the total HOME score in infancy (Braungart, in press). The Variety of Daily Stimulation scale is also the only HOME scale that shows heritability in early childhood.

Finding genetic contributions to the HOME in infancy is important for two reasons. First, the HOME is more objective than the questionnaires used in the studies discussed previously. This suggests that genetic effects on the family environment are not just in the minds of parents and children but in their behavior as well. Second, the finding is especially impressive because the HOME instrument makes it difficult to detect genetic effects using a child-based genetic design. As discussed earlier, a child-based genetic design can detect genetic effects only to the extent that the measure reflects genetic differences among children, not genetic differences among parents. The HOME, however, includes many items that are not specific to the child and thus cannot be expected to reflect genetic differences among siblings. For example, such items as numbers of books and of pets in the home correlate highly for the two children (for both nonadoptive and adoptive sibling pairs) and thus cannot display genetic effects. This is in contrast to items that are specific to each child, such as mother's response to the child's vocalizations and mother's punishment of child.

LYTTON'S OBSERVATIONAL TWIN STUDY

A small twin study by Hugh Lytton (1977, 1980) employed observational ratings of mothers interacting with their 2-year-old twins, although interview data were also included in the study's composite measures. The observational data suggested genetic effects for seven parental treatment variables: material rewards, amount of play, support of dependence, encouraging mature action, monitoring, use of reasoning, and play frequency. A follow-up study at age 9 also suggested genetic contributions to the twins' ratings of their parents' attitudes and practices (Lytton, Watts, & Dunn, 1986, 1988).

The most interesting feature of Lytton's study was its coding of parent-initiated actions, defined as parental actions that were not preceded by a child's action within the previous 10 seconds. These measures of parent-initiated actions were summarized in four categories: command/prohibition, suggestion, positive action, and negative action. Genetic effects emerged primarily for child-initiated rather than parent-initiated actions. This finding makes sense because the design is child-based, which means that genetic effects should primarily be observed for child-initiated interactions. A parent-based design, however, might show greater genetic effects for parent-initiated actions. Lytton's results also support the equal environments assumption of the twin method in the sense that parents respond to rather than create greater similarity in their children. This pioneering study is an exemplar of the type of research that is needed to understand the processes by which genetic factors contribute to environmental measures.

VIDEOTAPE OBSERVATIONS OF
MOTHER-CHILD INTERACTIONS IN CAP

The Colorado Adoption Project (CAP) provided the first reports of videotaped observations of mother-child interactions in a genetic design. Although such observations have their own methodological limitations, such as their artificiality and their brevity, they are at least more objective than questionnaires. Thus observational data make it possible to assess whether genetic influence on environmental measures is limited to subjective processes involved in questionnaire assessments.

In CAP, ratings were made from videotapes of mothers interacting with each of the nonadoptive and adoptive siblings when the child was 1, 2, and 3 years old for a subsample of the CAP siblings (Dunn & Plomin, 1986). In addition to its objectivity, an important feature of this measurement strategy is that, unlike the HOME, maternal behavior specific to each child is assessed. At each age, mother and one child were videotaped in three 5-minute sessions: a structured task (teaching), a moderately structure task (play with a specific set of toys), and an unstructured task (free play). Factor analysis of various behavioral counts and ratings yielded factors representing affection, control, and verbal responsiveness.

Nonadoptive and adoptive sibling correlations for these three factors at 1, 2, and 3 years of age are shown in Table 2.13. Despite the small sample sizes, the affection factor consistently shows nonadoptive correlations that are substantially greater than adoptive correlations. No genetic contribution is suggested for the control and verbal factors, with the exception of control at 3 years. Although the small sample size warrants caution in drawing conclusions, this caution is offset to some extent by the replication of results across the 3 years. As they stand, the results suggest that maternal affection is associated with genetic differences between children. Concerning the suggestion of genetic effects on control at 3 years, it should be noted that in contrast to the questionnaire studies that define control in terms of attitudes about rules and organization, control in this study is very different, referring to specific observable behaviors involving mothers' directiveness and intrusiveness.

In this series of reports, each child was videotaped interacting individually with his or her mother when the child was 1, 2, and 3 years old. In other words, the siblings were studied at the same age but at different measurement occasions separated on average by 2 years. The Colorado Adoption Project also included a subproject called the Colorado Sibling Study in which the siblings were studied at the same measurement occasion but at different ages (Dunn, Stocker, & Plomin, 1990). Children were videotaped

**TABLE 2.13** Correlations for Nonadoptive and Adoptive Siblings for Videotaped Observations of Mother-Child Interaction at 1, 2, and 3 Years of Age

| | | Sibling Correlations | |
|---|---|---|---|
| Factor | Age | Nonadoptive | Adoptive |
| Affection | 1 | .70 | .37 |
| | 2 | .60 | .31 |
| | 3 | .55 | -.05* |
| Control | 1 | .44 | .46 |
| | 2 | .09 | .22 |
| | 3 | .85 | .32* |
| Verbal | 1 | .48 | .43 |
| | 2 | .68 | .65 |
| | 3 | .30 | .29 |

SOURCE: Adapted from Dunn & Plomin (1986); Dunn, Plomin, & Daniels (1986); Dunn, Plomin, & Nettles (1985).
NOTE: The number of nonadoptive and adoptive sibling pairs were 32 and 14 at 1, 26 and 19 at 2, and 23 and 21 at 3.
* Nonadoptive sibling correlation significantly ($p < .05$) greater than adoptive sibling correlation.

interacting with their mother and sibling and mothers were interviewed about the siblings when older siblings were 7 years old on average and younger siblings were 4 (Rende, Slomkowski, Stocker, Fulker, & Plomin, 1992). The sibling adoption design comparing nonadoptive and adoptive sibling correlations was employed to investigate genetic effects.

As shown in Table 2.14, videotape ratings of maternal behavior indicated significant genetic contributions to control and attention, but not for affection and responsiveness. This finding supports the general finding of genetic effects on parental behavior in child-based genetic designs, but conflicts with previous studies in finding genetic effects for control but not warmth. As discussed above, CAP videotape analyses of these same nonadoptive and adoptive siblings showed genetic contributions to warmth but not control when each child was observed interacting with mother when the child was 1 and 2 years, although at 3 years genetic effects emerged for control (Dunn & Plomin, 1986). This discrep-

**TABLE 2.14** Correlations for Nonadoptive and Adoptive Siblings for Videotaped Observations of Mother-Child Interaction and Maternal Interviews When the Younger Sibling Was 4 and the Older Sibling 7 on Average

| Measure | Sibling Correlations | |
| --- | --- | --- |
| | *Nonadoptive* | *Adoptive* |
| *Video Observations* | | |
| Maternal Behavior | | |
| Control | .86 | .65* |
| Affection | .88 | .91 |
| Attention | .71 | .36* |
| Responsiveness | .95 | .94 |
| Sibling Behavior | | |
| Control | .36 | .28 |
| Competition | .66 | .46* |
| Conflict | .91 | .85 |
| Cooperation | .76 | .81 |
| *Unstructured Observations* | | |
| Sibling Behavior | | |
| Positive | .85 | .63* |
| Negative | .79 | .62* |
| *Maternal Interviews* | | |
| Sibling Behavior | | |
| Positive | .81 | .62* |
| Negative | .85 | .65* |

SOURCE: Adapted from Rende, Slomkowski, Stocker, Fulker, & Plomin (1992).
NOTE: The number of nonadoptive and adoptive sibling pairs were 67 and 57, respectively.
* Significant model-fitting estimate of heritability.

ancy could be due to the fact that the Rende et al. analysis involved observations of triads consisting of mother, older sibling, and younger sibling at a single measurement occasion, in contrast to the mother-child dyads that were assessed by Dunn and Plomin on two different measurement occasions, when each child was the same age. However, this hypothesis is somewhat less likely because the study by Lytton involved mother-twin-twin triads at the same time of measurement. Another possibility involves developmental specificity, in that infancy was the focus of the studies by Lytton and by Dunn and Plomin, whereas the children in the study by Rende et al. were primarily in middle childhood. This hypothesis receives some support from the finding by Dunn and Plomin of genetic effects on control at 3 years but not at 1 or 2 years. Nonetheless, until more observational research of this type is conducted, the most likely explanation lies with relatively small sample sizes and reduced statistical power.

The study by Rende et al. also included videotaped observations of siblings' behavior toward each other in structured and unstructured settings. Observations of sibling interaction in structured settings suggested only a modest role for genetic factors. However, observations of sibling behavior in unstructured settings suggested genetic effects for both positive and negative dimensions of sibling interaction. In general, sibling correlations are very high, which suggests that observations of mothers and siblings interacting at the same time in their home might be overwhelmed by situational factors that increase their resemblance and thus make it difficult to detect genetic effects. As indicated in Table 2.14, maternal interviews about sibling interactions yielded results comparable to those from the observations, showing significant heritability for both positive and negative dimensions. Estimates of heritability were scarcely affected after partialling out family constellation variables such as birth order and age spacing.

NEAD: A NEW OBSERVATIONAL STUDY

The pièce de résistance is the aforementioned NEAD project, which included six groups of adolescent siblings. In addition to its numerous questionnaire measures of family interactions, the study included videotapes of family members engaged in 10-minute discussions around topics of problems and conflicts. The behavior of each child and each parent was rated independently on 14 dimensions such as warmth, self-disclosure, involvement, assertiveness, and control. Model-fitting analyses yielded an average heritability of .21 for children's behavior toward mother, and .23 for children's behavior toward father (O'Connor, Hetherington, Reiss, & Plomin, in press). As expected for a child-based genetic design, the heritabilities for parents' behavior toward the siblings were much lower. Parents' behavior toward the children yielded an average heritability of .09 for mothers and .08 for fathers.

The 14 dimensions were aggregated into two composites, positivity and negativity, as part of a measurement model incorporated within the genetic model-fitting analysis. For parents' behavior toward the children, a control composite was also included. Table 2.15 presents the NEAD model-fitting results for these composites, which are error-free latent variables. The heritabilities of children's behavior toward their parents are significant and substantial and remarkably similar for behavior toward mother and toward father.

Parents' behavior toward their children also shows significant genetic influence for positivity and negativity. It is interesting that, at least for mothers, control yields a zero heritability. As noted in relation to the results for the 14 dimensions, parents' behavior toward their children shows less genetic influence than children's behavior toward their parents. As discussed earlier, low heritability for parental behavior makes sense given that the genetic design is child-based. If a similar study were conducted with adult twins interacting with their children, we would expect greater heritability for parental behavior and lower heritabilities for the behavior of the children.

## Summary

Beginning with Rowe's two original studies more than a decade ago, half a dozen twin and adoption studies converge on the conclusion that genetic factors play a role in children's perceptions of parenting. Evidence for genetic contributions emerges for all dimensions of children's perceptions of parenting with the interesting exception of control-related dimensions. Children's perceptions of their siblings' behavior toward them also shows genetic effects.

Genetic effects are not just limited to children's perceptions of their family environment. Parents' perceptions of their parenting

**TABLE 2.15** NEAD Model-Fitting Components of Variance for Composites of Videotaped Observations Derived From a Measurement Model

| Respondent | Target | Measure | $e_n^2$ | $e_s^2$ | $h^2$ |
|---|---|---|---|---|---|
| Child | Mother | Positivity | .35* | .06 | .59* |
| | | Negativity | .37* | .15 | .48* |
| Child | Father | Positivity | .36* | .00 | .64* |
| | | Negativity | .25* | .23* | .52* |
| Mother | Child | Positivity | .19* | .63* | .18* |
| | | Negativity | .29* | .34* | .38* |
| | | Control | .58* | .42* | .00 |
| Father | Child | Positivity | .19* | .63* | .18* |
| | | Negativity | .34* | .42* | .24* |
| | | Control | .25* | .51* | .24* |

SOURCE: Adapted from O'Connor, Hetherington, Reiss, & Plomin (in press).
NOTE: Model-fitting estimates of nonshared environment/error ($e_n^2$), shared environment ($e_s^2$), and heritability ($h^2$).

implicate genetic contributions even in child-based genetic designs (i.e., twins are the children in the family). In child-based genetic designs, genetic effects can be detected only to the extent that parents' perceptions of their parenting reflect genetically influenced characteristics of their children. Again, heritability seems stronger for dimensions of parenting other than control. Three studies using parent-based genetic designs—for example, when twins are parents rating their own parenting style—also show genetic effects, even for control-related dimensions.

Finally, evidence of genetic effects emerges from four observational studies of parenting and sibling behavior using child-based genetic designs. The results from these observational studies suggest that the genetic contribution to measures of the family environment is not limited to subjective processes involved in questionnaires. Genetic effects appear to be not just in the eye of the beholder but also in the behavior of the individual.

These same data provide strong evidence for the importance of nongenetic influence as well. However, it is not news that environmental measures are environmental; the news is that genetic factors contribute to environmental measures. For this reason, the focus has been on the genetic story. Nonetheless, one implication for environmental research is clear: Unless family environmental measures are studied using genetic designs, it cannot be safely assumed that such measures and their associations with outcome measures are truly environmental. This nature-nurture confound is especially profound for the vast majority of studies that involve genetically related family members. Implications of these findings are discussed in Chapter 5.

The following chapter continues to document the basic phenomenon of genetic effects on environmental measures. It tracks genetic effects beyond the family to other social environments such as friends, peers, teachers, and to other phenomena such as life events.

# 3

# The Nature of Nurture

## *The Environment Beyond the Family*

Is the role of genetic factors in environmental measures limited to measures of the family environment? Within families, individuals are genetically related. It is possible that this concatenation of genetic and environmental relatedness, which will be discussed in later chapters as passive genotype-environment correlation, leads to the finding of a genetic contribution. Are genetic effects found for environmental measures that go beyond interactions with relatives?

Although most research to date on the nature of nurture has focused on the family environment, evidence is beginning to mount that genetic factors also contribute to extrafamilial environmental measures. In this section, quantitative genetic research on peers, life events, and other extrafamilial environments is briefly described.

### Peers

The peer relations literature emphasizes associations between parenting and children's peer relations (Hartup, 1983; Rubin &

Sloman, 1984). The evidence from the previous chapter on the contribution of genetic factors to parenting suggests that genetic factors may in part be responsible for this association (Rowe, 1989). For example, children may be sociable both with their parents and their peers. In this way, genetic factors that influence sociability could contribute to associations between such familial and extrafamilial variables. Moreover, a fundamental feature of peers is that they are outside the family. Children do not choose their parents and siblings, but they do to some extent choose their peers and are chosen by them. This selection process opens up new opportunities for a genetic contribution. The focus of this section is characteristics of the peer group rather than popularity as indexed, for example, by a peer-nomination measure of sociometric status. Popularity seems more directly a measure of the child than of the child's environment. One twin study of sociometric ratings of popularity found evidence of genetic influence; twin correlations were .70 for identical twins and .52 for fraternal twins (Roff, Sells, & Golden, 1972).

The first indication that genetic factors contribute to characteristics of children's peer groups came from analyses of the SIDE. As discussed in the previous chapter, the SIDE asks each child to rate directly the relative differential treatment comparing the child and the sibling. The relative ratings for each child are converted to absolute differences that indicate the extent of differential treatment independent of which sibling received more or less. The previous chapter presented results that showed genetic effects for the SIDE parental and sibling scales in a twin study (Baker & Daniels, 1990), in a sibling adoption study (Daniels & Plomin, 1985), and in the NEAD twin and stepfamily study (Pike et al., 1993). The SIDE also includes three scales that assess characteristics of peer groups: College Orientation, Delinquency, and Popularity. As indicated in Table 3.1, the twin study of adults shows strong genetic effects for the SIDE peer scales, stronger than for the SIDE parental and sibling scales (Table 2.3). The average effect size comparing the mean absolute differences for identical and fraternal twins in Table 2.3 was .46 for parents and .35 for siblings,

**TABLE 3.1**   MZ and DZ Within-Pair Differences for Retrospective Reports of Adult Twins on the SIDE Peer Scales

| SIDE Scales | MZ diff (SD) | | DZ diff (SD) |
|---|---|---|---|
| Peer College Orientation | .31 (.38) | * | .65 (.42) |
| Peer Delinquency | .37 (.45) | * | .64 (.51) |
| Peer Popularity | .43 (.49) | * | .77 (.52) |

SOURCE: Adapted from Baker & Daniels (1990).
NOTE: Sample includes 139-161 MZ pairs and 61-74 DZ pairs.
* Mean of MZ difference significantly ($p < .05$) lower than mean of DZ.

**TABLE 3.2**   MZ and DZ Within-Pair Differences on the SIDE Peer Scales in Adolescent Twins

| SIDE Scales | Twin 1 | | | Twin 2 | | |
|---|---|---|---|---|---|---|
| | MZ diff (SD) | | DZ diff (SD) | MZ diff (SD) | | DZ diff (SD) |
| Peer College Orientation | .18 (.28) | * | .37 (.41) | .24 (.35) | * | .46 (.43) |
| Peer Delinquency | .21 (.32) | * | .46 (.49) | .24 (.31) | * | .50 (.44) |
| Peer Popularity | .19 (.28) | * | .40 (.37) | .22 (.33) | * | .38 (.37) |

SOURCE: Adapted from Pike, Manke, Hetherington, Reiss, & Plomin (1993).
NOTE: Sample include 93 MZ pairs and 98 DZ pairs.
* Mean of MZ difference significantly ($p < .05$) lower than mean of DZ.

which indicates that identical and fraternal twins differ by less than half a standard deviation. From Table 3.1, the average effect size for the peer scales is .70.

Strong evidence for genetic effects on the SIDE peer scales also comes from the NEAD twin results (Table 3.2). The average effect size is .57. NEAD also includes non-twin full siblings in non-divorced families. These full siblings show larger differences on the SIDE peer scales than the DZ twins. This suggests, not surprisingly, that twins, both MZ and DZ, experience more similar peer groups than non-twin siblings. An interesting side issue is that, for the full siblings in nondivorced families, the older children within each sibling pair perceived greater differences in peer characteristics than did the younger members of the sibling pairs.

**TABLE 3.3**  Nonadoptive and Adoptive Within-Pair Differences on the SIDE Peer Scales for Adolescents and Young Adults

| SIDE Scales | Nonadoptive diff (SD) | | Adoptive diff (SD) |
|---|---|---|---|
| Peer College Orientation | .72 (.36) | * | .84 (.38) |
| Peer Delinquency | .80 (.48) | * | .96 (.50) |
| Peer Popularity | .73 (.45) | * | .97 (.45) |

SOURCE: Adapted from Daniels & Plomin (1985).
NOTE: Sample includes 115-149 pairs of nonadoptive siblings and 106-166 pairs of adoptive siblings.
* Mean of nonadoptive siblings significantly lower than mean of adoptive siblings.

**TABLE 3.4**  Within-Pair Differences for Stepfamily Full Siblings and Unrelated Siblings on the SIDE Peer Scales in Adolescents

| SIDE Scales | Older Child | | Younger Child | |
| | Full Sib diff (SD) | Un. Sib diff (SD) | Full Sib diff (SD) | Un. Sib diff (SD) |
|---|---|---|---|---|
| Peer College Orientation | .86 (.49) | .72 (.48) | .53 (.43) | .60 (.49) |
| Peer Delinquency | .84 (.50) | .75 (.67) | .57 (.42) | .64 (.54) |
| Peer Popularity | .64 (.46) | .67 (.48) | .53 (.45) | .62 (.51) |

SOURCE: Adapted from Pike, Manke, Hetherington, Reiss, & Plomin (1993).
NOTE: Sample includes 182 pairs of full siblings and 130 pairs of unrelated siblings, all in stepfamilies.

The sibling adoption study of Daniels and Plomin also shows substantial genetic effects, as indicated in Table 3.3. The only exception to this picture of substantial genetic effects comes from the stepfamily design of NEAD, as shown in Table 3.4. Differences for unrelated siblings were not significantly greater than differences for full siblings for the three SIDE peer scales. As noted in the previous chapter, the within-family processes in stepfamilies may differ from those in nondivorced families. However, the aberrant results of the stepfamily design may be limited to the relative ratings of the SIDE. The NEAD project included a traditional questionnaire in which mothers and fathers rated characteristics of their children's peers (Manke, McGuire, Reiss, Hetherington,

**TABLE 3.5**  NEAD Sibling Correlations and Heritabilities for Parental
Ratings of Siblings' Peers

| Scale | MZ | DZ | FN | FS | HS | US | Heritability |
|-------|----|----|----|----|----|----|--------------|
| Peer College Orientation | | | | | | | |
| Mother | .89 | .44 | .41 | .25 | .30 | .03 | .85* |
| Father | .86 | .66 | .43 | .31 | .40 | .13 | .73* |
| Peer Delinquency | | | | | | | |
| Mother | .87 | .58 | .57 | .50 | .50 | .17 | .70* |
| Father | .78 | .61 | .56 | .54 | .47 | .42 | .49* |
| Peer Substance Abuse | | | | | | | |
| Mother | .95 | .46 | .52 | .39 | .58 | .22 | .72* |
| Father | .92 | .86 | .51 | .53 | .45 | .09 | .74* |
| Peer Popularity | | | | | | | |
| Mother | .77 | .41 | .40 | .14 | .30 | .00 | .73* |
| Father | .80 | .50 | .15 | .27 | .52 | .15 | .62* |

SOURCE: Adapted from Manke, McGuire, Reiss, Hetherington, & Plomin (1993).
NOTE: MZ = identical twins in nondivorced families, DZ = fraternal twins in nondivorced
families, FN = full siblings in nondivorced families, FS = full siblings in stepfamilies, HS = half
siblings in stepfamilies, and US = unrelated children in stepfamilies. Sample sizes are 93 MZ
pairs, 98 DZ pairs, 95 FN pairs, 182 FS pairs, 109 HS pairs, and 130 US pairs.
* $p < .05$

& Plomin, 1993). As shown in Table 3.5, for both mothers' and
fathers' ratings, these peer measures yield heritabilities twice as
great as heritabilities for NEAD measures of the family environment reported in Table 2.7.

In summary, ratings of characteristics of adolescents' peer groups
yield surprisingly strong evidence for genetic involvement. Spec-
ulation as to why peer measures show such high heritability is left
for Chapter 5.

## Friends and Teachers

Social environments outside the family include friends and
teachers as well as peers. In NEAD children rated positive and

**TABLE 3.6** NEAD Sibling Correlations and Heritabilities for Child Ratings of Friends and Teachers

| Scale | MZ | DZ | FN | FS | HS | US | Heritability |
|-------|------|------|------|------|------|------|------|
| Friend | | | | | | | |
| Positive | .31 | .21 | .14 | .14 | −.07 | .04 | .31* |
| Negative | .04 | .06 | .19 | .16 | .07 | .08 | .06 |
| Teacher | | | | | | | |
| Positive | .45 | .20 | .17 | .02 | .18 | .14 | .38* |
| Negative | .17 | .06 | .10 | .23 | .07 | .05 | .21 |

SOURCE: Adapted from Manke, McGuire, Reiss, Hetherington, & Plomin (1993).
NOTE: MZ = identical twins in nondivorced families, DZ = fraternal twins in nondivorced families, FN = full siblings in nondivorced families, FS = full siblings in stepfamilies, HS = half siblings in stepfamilies, and US = unrelated children in stepfamilies. Sample sizes are 93 MZ pairs, 98 DZ pairs, 95 FN pairs, 182 FS pairs, 109 HS pairs, and 130 US pairs.
* $p < .05$

negative aspects of their interactions with a best friend and with a teacher (Manke et al., 1993). The results, summarized in Table 3.6, indicate significant genetic effects for both friend and teacher for the positive dimension but not for the negative dimension, which shows little sibling resemblance for any group. Positive and negative aspects of interactions with parents and siblings do not appear to show this pattern of effects in the studies reviewed in the previous chapter. Moreover, the same measure in the NEAD was completed by children concerning their sibling and heritability was similar (about .20) for both the positive and negative dimensions. Together, these findings suggest that positive dimensions may show greater heritability than negative dimensions for extrafamilial relationships but not familial relationships. If this hypothesis survives replication, Loehlin (personal communication, January 31, 1993) has suggested a possible explanation. Positive judgments of people outside the family may reflect continued samples of interactions with them, which might be the result of our own enduring characteristics. In contrast, our negative judgments may be based on some isolated, perhaps almost random, behavior that we happen to have observed.

## Social Support

Social support is increasingly used as a measure of the social environment outside the family. In gerontology, for example, social support has become a defining characteristic of "successful aging" (Rowe & Kahn, 1987). It refers to the intensiveness and extensiveness of the network of social relationships that surround a person as well as the perceived adequacy of the network (Berkman, 1983). A genetic analysis of social support has been reported from SATSA, a study of middle-aged adults described in the previous chapter (Bergeman, Plomin, Pedersen, McClearn, & Nesselroade, 1990). Nine items from a modified version of the Interview Schedule for Social Interaction (Henderson, Duncan-Jones, Byrne, & Scott, 1980) were employed and yielded two scales: quality (perceived adequacy) and quantity or frequency of interactions with relatives and friends. Twin correlations, shown in Table 3.7, indicate significant heritability for the quality scale, but not for the quantity scale. It seems odd that perceptions of the sheer quantity of social support relationships show no heritability in this study. One might expect, for example, that quantity of relationships is related to sociability, which is one of the most highly heritable personality traits. A follow-up study using a revised measure of social support is underway in SATSA.

A study of female twins from 17 to 53 years of age also found evidence for a genetic contribution to social support (Kessler, Kendler, Heath, Neale, & Eaves, 1992). As shown in Table 3.8, significant genetic influence emerged for quality of support from relatives and friends and a single item that asked whether the subject has a close and confiding relationship. As in the SATSA report, single-item measures of the quantity of interactions with relatives and friends showed no heritability, although items assessing frequency of church attendance and club attendance were significantly heritable.

In summary, these first two studies of social support suggest that genetic factors make a contribution to individual differences in perceptions of support. An important implication of this finding is that the well-documented association between social sup-

**TABLE 3.7**  Twin Correlations and Heritabilities for Adult Twins' Ratings of Social Support

| Measure | MZA | MZT | DZA | DZT | Model-Fitting Heritability |
|---|---|---|---|---|---|
| Quality (perceived adequacy) | .19 | .34 | .21 | .05 | .30* |
| Quantity | .32 | .36 | .22 | .40 | .00 |

SOURCE: Adapted from Bergeman, Plomin, Pedersen, McClearn, & Nesselroade (1990).
NOTE: Sample sizes are 57-59 for MZA, 76-80 for MZT, 101-110 for DZA, and 110-117 for DZT.
* $p < .05$

**TABLE 3.8**  Twin Correlations and Heritabilities for Adult Female Twins' Ratings of Social Support

| Measure | MZT | DZT | Model-Fitting Heritability |
|---|---|---|---|
| Perceived spouse support | .22 | .25 | .00 |
| Perceived relative support | .47 | .30 | .28* |
| Perceived friend support | .30 | .11 | .32* |
| Confidant | .50 | .12 | .50* |
| Frequency of interaction with relatives | .42 | .39 | .00 |
| Frequency of interaction with friends | .23 | .32 | .00 |
| Frequency of church attendance | .80 | .62 | .36* |
| Frequency of club attendance | .52 | .23 | .52* |

SOURCE: Adapted from Kessler, Kendler, Heath, Neale, & Eaves (1992).
NOTE: Sample sizes are 458 MZ pairs and 353 DZ pairs.
* $p < .05$

port and reduced risk of psychopathology (Cohen & Wills, 1985) might be mediated genetically. This topic will be taken up again in Chapter 4, which considers genetic mediation between environmental measures and behavioral measures.

## Life Events

Life events is a category of extrafamilial environmental measures used in more than a thousand studies (Holmes, 1979). SATSA included a measure of life events based on the Social Readjustment

Rating Scale (Holmes & Rahe, 1967) modified for older individuals (Persson, 1980). Typical life events items ask about marital and work difficulties, financial problems, illnesses and injuries, and other crises such as being robbed or assaulted. In SATSA, a total life events score was constructed by summing each reported event weighted by the average importance assigned to the event by all individuals who completed the questionnaire. Table 3.9 lists SATSA twin correlations for this measure. These results differ somewhat from earlier published results (Plomin, Lichtenstein, Pedersen, McClearn, & Nesselroade, 1990) because zygosities of a few SATSA twins have been changed as a result of new zygosity diagnoses based on genetic markers from blood. As shown in the first row of Table 3.9, the pattern of correlations for the four groups of twins implicates a genetic contribution to total life events. The model-fitting estimate of heritability is 31%. However, an odd aspect of the results is the high MZA correlation, which is higher than the MZT correlation.

Finding genetic effects on life events implies that such events do not just happen capriciously to individuals. Life events happen (or are perceived to happen) to some people more than others. To some extent, this "bad luck" is related to genetically influenced characteristics of individuals. If this reasoning is correct, it should follow that those events in which the individual is involved and has some control show greater heritability than events that are out of the hands of the individual. Examples of events that involve the person include serious conflicts with child, major deterioration in financial status, divorce, and paying a fine for a minor violation of the law. Events in which the respondent is less involved include events that happen to others such as serious illness in child, forced change in residence, mental illness of spouse, and death of siblings or friends.

SATSA results, shown in the second and third rows in Table 3.9, confirm this expectation. Events that were judged to involve the respondent to a greater degree show greater heritability than events that happen to others. Heritability estimates are 30% for events to self and 18% for events to others.

It might seem odd that events that occur to others such as serious illness of one's child show any genetic contribution at all.

**TABLE 3.9**  Twin Correlations and Heritabilities for Older Adult Twins'
Ratings of Life Events

| Life Events Scale | MZA | MZT | DZA | DZT | Model-Fitting Heritability |
|---|---|---|---|---|---|
| Total score | .43 | .24 | .07 | .19 | .31* |
| Events to self | .27 | .27 | .21 | .10 | .30* |
| Events to others | .22 | .11 | .06 | .15 | .18* |

SOURCE: Unpublished data.
NOTE: * $p < .05$
Sample sizes are 45-49 for MZA, 90-98 for MZT, 107-125 for DZA, and 112-127 for DZT.

However, it is possible that events such as familial illness entail some genetic effects. Another possibility lies in the use of perceptions of life events. Genetic factors involved in perceptions that filter through a person's memories, feelings, and personality might dispose some dour individuals to consider their child's illness as a "serious illness" in contrast to other people who would not label the same illness as serious.

The life events literature has also made a distinction between positive and negative events. A keystone of the original Holmes and Rahe life events instrument was the assumption that stress is incurred by positive events such as marriage as well as by negative events such as divorce. Subsequent research has indicated that negative events are more predictive of problems than positive events (Thoits, 1983). Nonetheless, genetic analysis yields similar results for positive and negative events. Model-fitting heritabilities were .31 for positive events and .36 for negative events (Plomin, Lichtenstein, et al., 1990).

In SATSA, analyses of longitudinal follow-up testing 3 and 6 years after the original wave of testing are in progress. Preliminary analyses indicate that these data confirm the basic findings reported in Table 3.9 as do the results of three other twin studies. One of the two replication studies involved reared-apart adult twins (Moster, 1990, cited in McGue, Bouchard, Lykken, & Finkel, 1991). Even stronger results were found than in SATSA. Personal events were substantially more heritable ($h^2 = .51$) than events to others ($h^2 = .18$). The second replication was a large classical twin study comparing MZT and DZT from 17 to 55 years old using a measure of life events during the past year (Kendler, Neale, Kessler, Heath, & Eaves, in press). As shown in the first row of Table 3.10, the heritability estimate for the total life events score is significant. The results also confirm the SATSA finding that personal events show greater heritability than events to others. As shown in Table 3.10, the categories of events to self showed significant heritability but the categories of events to others did not. For example, the greatest heritability was found for the respondent's own financial problems, whereas death, illness/injury, and crises of others showed nonsignificant heritability. It is noteworthy that the results were generally similar for males and females, although marital difficulties appeared to show genetic effects for males but not females. Also, similarity of childhood environment did not systematically relate to twin resemblance for life events. Frequency of contact as adults significantly predicted twin similarity, but controlling for frequency of contact did not alter the genetic findings. A third small twin study also shows genetic influence (Wierzbicki, 1989).

Although the results in Table 3.10 show only modest heritability for "marital difficulties," a recent twin study of divorce involving 1,516 pairs of twins suggested substantial heritability (McGue & Lykken, 1992). When one twin has been divorced, the risk of divorce for the co-twin is .45 for MZ twins and .30 for DZ twins. Tetrachoric correlations that assume an underlying continuum of liability were .55 for MZ twins and .16 for DZ twins, yielding an estimate of .53 for heritability of divorce liability in a model-fitting analysis. A preliminary report of another twin study of divorce suggests less heritability, although the sample employed showed unusually low rates of divorce (Turkheimer, Lovett, Robinette, & Gottesman, 1992).

One twin study of 68 MZ and 109 DZ pairs did not replicate these findings for life events, but this study was different from the others in two respects (McGuffin & Katz, 1993). A checklist of 12 common categories of events during the preceding 6 months was employed. A second difference is that the sample was selected for diagnoses of depression. Perhaps for this reason, the reported frequency of life events was very high, about 70%, for both the depressed probands and their co-twins. No apparent concordance

**TABLE 3.10** Twin Correlations and Heritabilities for Adult Twins' Ratings of Life Events

| Life Events Scale | MZT | DZT | Model-Fitting Heritability |
|---|---|---|---|
| Total score | .43 | .31 | .26* |
| Events to self: | | | |
| financial problems | .44 | .12 | .39* |
| robbed/assaulted | .31 | .19 | .33* |
| illness/injury | .28 | .00 | .21* |
| interpersonal difficulties | .39 | .30 | .18* |
| marital difficulties | .13 | .09 | .14* |
| work difficulties | .33 | .27 | — |
| Events to others: | | | |
| illness/injury | .35 | .30 | — |
| crises | .39 | .33 | — |
| death | .47 | .44 | — |

SOURCE: Adapted from Kendler, Neale, Kessler, Heath, & Eaves (in press).
NOTE: Sample sizes are 890 MZT and 1425 DZT. The missing heritabilities were not calculated because model-fitting indicated that these heritabilities were not significant.
* $p < .05$

emerged for either MZ or DZ twins for a dichotomous measure of whether any life events were reported, which seems odd given that the frequency of life events was high for both probands and co-twins. When the number of events was used as a dimension rather than a dichotomy, familial resemblance was observed but correlations were similar for MZ twins ($r = .37$) and DZ twins ($r = .33$). The results were not analyzed separately for events to self and events to others. Similar results were observed when subjective distress in response to these events was analyzed.

Although there is not agreement concerning the best way to assess life events, there is widespread dissatisfaction with traditional questionnaire measures (e.g., Paykel, 1983). Finding genetic effects on questionnaire measures of life events justifies the need for research using more expensive instruments such as interviews. One family study of neurotic depression (McGuffin, Katz, & Bebbington, 1988) included an interview measure of life events, the Life Events and Difficulties Schedule (Brown & Harris, 1978).

Familial resemblance was found for life events, although it remains to be seen whether familial resemblance for this widely used interview measure is due to genetic factors.

Another interesting direction for research in this area is to investigate daily hassles, which appear to be more strongly associated with adjustment than do major life events (Holahan & Holahan, 1987). Although no studies of this type have been reported, a measure was constructed as part of the Colorado Adoption Project to assess the stressfulness of first grade (Rende & Plomin, 1991). Using a sibling adoption design that compares nonadoptive and adoptive siblings, no evidence was found for a genetic contribution to total number of events or a composite rating of upsettingness for either 7-year-olds' self-ratings or their parents' ratings (Rende, in press). For the child ratings, correlations were about .05 for both adoptive and nonadoptive siblings. This suggests that siblings in the same family experience entry into formal schooling quite differently. For parent reports, correlations were about .25 for both types of siblings. This might indicate some shared environmental influence, although it is more likely to be due to the fact that a single rater, the parent, rated both children. Although it is noteworthy that no evidence for heritability emerged from this first study of stress related to the first year of school, interpretation of these findings should await replication.

Finally, accidents represent an important category of life events for children. Accidents may not be entirely accidental (Matheny, 1988). A twin analysis of injuries during the first 3 years of life yielded MZ and DZ liability correlations of .51 and .13, respectively, for a sample of 314 twin pairs (Phillips & Matheny, 1993). The low fraternal twin correlation suggests that these genetic effects operate nonadditively. A model-fitting estimate of heritability of accident liability was .51.

As in the case of social support, these first analyses of life events show genetic effects and raise the question whether genetic factors might mediate associations between such environmental measures and outcomes. This question is addressed in Chapter 4.

## Others Aspects of Extrafamilial Environments

The extrafamilial environment is vast and extends far beyond peers, friends, social support, and life events. Glimpses of future directions for genetic research in this area can be seen in isolated studies of classroom environment, work environment, television viewing, drug exposure, socioeconomic status, and education.

### CLASSROOM ENVIRONMENT

The Classroom Environment Scale (CES; Trickett & Moos, 1974) was analyzed in a twin study of 89 MZ pairs, 49 same-sex DZ pairs, and 65 same-sex non-twin sibling pairs from 16 to 45 years of age (Jang, 1993). The CES is a 90-item true-false questionnaire that assesses perceptions of the classroom. In this study, the twins were instructed to respond retrospectively "to whichever teacher or class they could best recall" (p. 99). The CES yields nine scales and three second-order dimensions similar to the FES. For example, the Affiliation scale includes the item, "Students in this class get to know each other really well."

The results for the CES are summarized in Table 3.11. Because the twins probably rated different classes and perhaps different schools, it is surprising that any twin resemblance was found. Four of the scales suggested a genetic contribution: Task Orientation, Rule Clarity, Teacher Control, and Innovation. It is interesting that the other scales, which included "warmth" scales such as Affiliation and Teacher Support, showed effects of shared environment rather than genetics.

This study also included the FES (see Chapter 2) and a measure called the Environmental Response Inventory (ERI; McKenchie, 1974). The ERI attempts to assess personality and attitudinal contributions to "environmental dispositions." Items include interests ("I like amusement parks") and attitudes ("Machines increase man's freedom"). The 184 items are scored on eight scales: pastoralism, urbanism, environmental adaption, stimulus seeking, environmental

**TABLE 3.11** Twin Correlations for Young Adult Twins' Retrospective Ratings of Classroom Environment

| Classroom Environment Measure | MZT | DZT | Non-Twin Siblings | Model-Fitting Heritability |
|---|---|---|---|---|
| Relationship Dimension | | | | |
| Involvement | .18 | .37 | .12 | .00 |
| Affiliation | .28 | .29 | .26 | .00 |
| Teacher Support | .18 | .21 | .14 | .00 |
| Personal Growth | | | | |
| Task Orientation | .26 | .07 | .23 | .32 |
| Competition | .22 | .24 | −.05 | .00 |
| System Maintenance | | | | |
| Order and Organization | .37 | .35 | .12 | .00 |
| Rule Clarity | .23 | .05 | .15 | .20 |
| Teacher Control | .31 | .02 | .11 | .29 |
| Innovation | .28 | .14 | .12 | .28 |

SOURCE: Adapted from Jang (1993).
NOTE: Sample sizes are 89 MZT, 49 same-sex DZT, and 65 same-sex non-twin sibling pairs.

trust, antiquarianism, need for privacy, and mechanical orientation. These seem like dimensions of personality and the results are much like those for personality questionnaires. The average correlations are .44 for MZ twins and .17 for DZ twins; the average correlation for non-twin siblings is somewhat higher (.28) than for DZ twins. Model-fitting heritability estimates ranged from .43 to .61 with the exception of three scales that showed negligible heritability and substantial shared environmental influence: Environmental adaption, environmental trust, and need for privacy.

WORK ENVIRONMENT

For working adults, almost half of their waking hours are spent at the workplace. The sheer quantity of time spent in this environment, as well as its potential impact, warrants greater consideration as a force in adult development. A report from SATSA for twins who had been employed (Hershberger, Lichtenstein, Knox, & McClearn, in press) assessed perceptions of organizational climate using the Work Environment Scale (WES), which includes scales such as involvement, peer cohesion, autonomy, work pressure, and control (Moos, 1981). In addition, an annoyance scale was created from 18 items concerning the annoyance caused by such physical stressors as noise, odors, and uncleanliness. An unrotated first principal component yielded a general factor of perceived organizational climate. The twin/adoption results from SATSA are presented for this measure in the first row of Table 3.12. The MZA correlation is significant and the pattern of other correlations also suggests genetic effects. The heritability estimate (.30) is significant. Four of the nine WES primary scales also indicate significant heritability: supervisor support, autonomy, work pressure, and clarity. In addition, the annoyance scale showed significant heritability, in contrast to the finding of no heritability for a scale of work difficulties described in the previous section (Kendler et al., in press). Although it has been suggested that education is an important aspect of an individual's work attitudes (Copranzano & James, 1990), covarying education scarcely changed the genetic results.

A possible mechanism for genetic effects on work environments is selection. Contributing to this selection might be vocational interests, intelligence, and personality. The ambitious study of Kohn and Schooler (1983) focuses on the role of personality. For example, self-directed individuals move into complex jobs and the complexity of their work enhances their self-directedness.

CHILDREN'S TELEVISION VIEWING

Children's television viewing has been used as an environmental measure in thousands of studies that investigated the consequences of television viewing (Pearl, Bouthilet, & Lazar, 1982). Despite a huge research effort to investigate its consequences, little is known about the causes of individual differences in children's television viewing (Bryant, 1990). It is not merely a matter of parental restrictions, because 70% of parents put no restrictions on the amount of time their children watch television (Lyle & Hoffman, 1972). This makes it more plausible to consider characteristics of children, including genetically influenced characteristics, among

**TABLE 3.12**  Twin Correlations and Heritabilities for Older Adult Twins'
Ratings of Work Environment

| Work Environment Measure | MZA | MZT | DZA | DZT | Model-Fitting Heritability |
|---|---|---|---|---|---|
| General Factor | .35 | .46 | .02 | .24 | .30* |
| Involvement | -.02 | .22 | .09 | .36 | .00 |
| Peer Cohesion | .27 | .23 | .19 | .13 | .13 |
| Supervisor Support | .24 | .35 | .02 | .18 | .20* |
| Autonomy | .28 | .33 | .06 | .02 | .26* |
| Task Orientation | .12 | .30 | -.06 | .25 | .02 |
| Work Pressure | .20 | .27 | .27 | -.02 | .25* |
| Clarity | .27 | .34 | -.01 | .15 | .23* |
| Control | .05 | .19 | .14 | .14 | .02 |
| Innovation | .00 | .21 | -.07 | -.14 | .03 |
| Annoyance | .41 | .36 | -.01 | .24 | .27* |

SOURCE: Adapted from Hershberger, Lichtenstein, Knox, & McClearn (in press).
NOTE: Sample sizes are 43-50 for MZA, 79-95 for MZT, 79-99 for DZA, and 88-95 for DZT, except for the annoyance scale for which the number of twin pairs was 25, 61, 61, and 52, respectively.
* $p < .05$.

the provenances of this measure. Individual differences in the amount of television viewing in children were investigated at 3, 4, and 5 years of age as part of the Colorado Adoption Project (Plomin, Corley, DeFries, & Fulker, 1990). Results from a sibling adoption analysis are summarized in Table 3.13. They show substantial heritability on individual differences in television viewing at 3 and 4 years.

Parent-offspring comparisons also supported the hypothesis of heritability, despite the different processes likely to be involved in television viewing of adult parents and their young children. Most impressive are the significant correlations between biological mothers and their adopted-away offspring at 4 and 5 years, as shown in Table 3.14. Genetic effects are also suggested by the greater parent-offspring correlations in nonadoptive families as compared to adoptive families, especially for mothers. Model-fitting heritability estimates are listed in Table 3.14, but it should be noted that these estimates assume isomorphism between the child measure and

**TABLE 3.13** Correlations for Nonadoptive and Adoptive Siblings for Amount of Television Viewing at 3, 4, and 5 Years of Age

| Age | Sibling Correlations | | Model-Fitting Heritability |
|-----|------------|----------|------------|
| | *Nonadoptive* | *Adoptive* | |
| 3 | .45 | .18 | .54* |
| 4 | .57 | .26 | .62* |
| 5 | .43 | .34 | .19 |

SOURCE: Plomin, R., Corley, R., DeFries, J. C., & Fulker, D. W. (1990). Individual differences in television viewing in early childhood: Nature as well as nurture. *Psychological Science, 1,* 371-377. Reprinted with permission of Cambridge University Press.
NOTE: The numbers of nonadoptive and adoptive sibling pairs were 70-95 and 70-82, respectively.
* $p < .05$.

adult measure. They underestimate the genetic contribution to children's television viewing to the extent that genetic effects differ in childhood and adulthood, which is probably why these parent-offspring heritability estimates are lower than the estimates from the sibling adoption design (Table 3.13). Similar results for the sibling adoption design and the parent-offspring adoption design have been reported in a follow-up analysis at 7 years of age (Corley & Coon, 1991).

## EXPOSURE TO DRUGS

Exposure to an environment does not imply that the environment will have an effect. Exposure to drugs (in contrast to actual drug use) is a good example. A study of 1,626 pairs of twins from the Vietnam Era Twin Registry found significant heritability for exposure to drugs, that is, reported opportunity to use marijuana, stimulants, sedatives, cocaine, opiates, and psychedelics (Tsuang et al., 1992). Heritability was stronger and more consistent for exposure to drugs than for actual use of the drugs.

## SOCIOECONOMIC STATUS AND EDUCATION

Parental education and socioeconomic status (SES) are among the most widely used indices of the home environment in studies

**TABLE 3.14** Correlations Between Biological, Adoptive, and Nonadoptive Parents and Their Children for Amount of Television Viewing at 3, 4, and 5 Years of Age

| Age | Biological | | Adoptive | | Nonadoptive | | Model-Fitting Heritability |
|-----|---------|---------|---------|---------|---------|---------|------------|
|     | Mothers | Fathers | Mothers | Fathers | Mothers | Fathers |            |
| 3   | −.01    | .18     | .07     | .09     | .30*    | .23*    | .07        |
| 4   | .15*    | .25*    | .12*    | .21*    | .31*    | .19*    | .13*       |
| 5   | .15*    | .12     | .16*    | .11     | .32*    | .11*    | .12*       |

SOURCE: Plomin, R., Corley, R., DeFries, J. C., & Fulker, D. W. (1990). Individual differences in television viewing in early childhood: Nature as well as nurture. *Psychological Science, 1,* 371-377. Reprinted with permission of Cambridge University Press.
NOTE: Ns for the six columns of data, respectively, are 216-221, 43-46, 217-223, 212-218, 221-228, and 224-231.
* p < .05.

of children's development. Nonetheless, these variables are included in this chapter on extrafamilial influences because they are important aspects of adults' own environments, regardless of whether the adults are parents. Rarely is the possibility of genetic effects considered, despite two well-established facts. Education and SES correlate greater than .50 with IQ (Jensen, 1980), and IQ is among the most highly heritable behavioral traits (Plomin & Neiderhiser, 1992b).

Both SES and education show genetic effects. For example, a study of 1,900 pairs of 50-year-old male twins yielded MZ and DZ twin correlations of .42 and .21, respectively, for occupational status, and .54 and .30 for income (Fulker & Eysenck, 1979; Taubman, 1976). An adoption study of occupational status yielded a correlation of .20 between biological fathers and their adult adopted-away sons (2,467 pairs; Teasdale, 1979). A study of 99 pairs of adopted-apart siblings yielded a correlation of .22 for occupational status (Teasdale & Owen, 1981). These studies, as well as more recent research from Norway (Tambs, Sundet, Magnus, & Berg, 1989) and Sweden (Lichtenstein & Pedersen, 1991; Lichtenstein, Pedersen, & McClearn, 1992) are consistent with a heritability of about .40 for occupational status. Years of schooling also shows substantial heritability in these studies. For example, MZ and DZ twin correlations are typically about .75 and .50, respectively, suggesting that heritability is about 50% (e.g., Taubman, 1976).

## Summary

In the previous chapter, genetic contributions were found for various aspects of the family environment, the focal point of environmental research in developmental psychology. This evidence included both child-based and parent-based twin and adoption studies of child and adult perceptions of family environment as well as observational studies. Recent research on extrafamilial environments, reviewed in this chapter, also implicates genetic factors.

This research finds that genetic factors play a role in measures of peers, friends, teachers, social support, life events, accidents, classroom environment, work environment, television viewing, exposure to drugs, education, and SES. There were two reasons for presenting this two-chapter litany of studies. The first was to describe the phenomenon that needs to be explained: Genetic effects emerge consistently from genetic research on a wide range of measures that have traditionally been regarded as measures of the environment. The second reason was to pick up hints about the processes by which genetic factors come to be involved in measures of the environment. Why do some environmental measures show less heritability than others? For example, in child-based genetic designs, why do measures of parental control show less heritability than other measures of parenting? Why are genetic effects so strong for measures of peer characteristics? In addition, some of these studies have begun to explore the question of how genetic factors become involved in environmental measures by investigating correlates of environmental measures, which is the topic of the following chapter.

This two-chapter review updates a 1991 "target" article in *Behavioral and Brain Sciences* that first pulled together research on this topic. The target article concluded:

> In summary, it is remarkable that research reported to date, using diverse measures and methods, so consistently converges on the conclusion that genetic influence is significant and substantial on widely used measures of the environment. (Plomin & Bergeman, 1991a, p. 386)

The target article was published with 30 commentaries and a response to the commentaries (Plomin & Bergeman, 1991b). Of the 30 commentaries, only 5 (Baumrind, Bookstein, Hirsch, Schonemann, Thelen) explicitly disagreed with the conclusion that genetic factors contribute to measures of the environment. However, rather than providing a plausible alternative explanation for these findings, these commentaries chose to discount them altogether. Their theme and the theme of more recent papers (e.g., Baumrind, 1993; Hoffman, 1991) was to deny that we are able to detect genetic effects on anything, let alone measures of the environment. The rocky relationship between such environmentalism and quantitative genetic research is discussed in several recent papers (Goldsmith, 1993; Rowe & Waldman, 1993; Rutter et al., 1993). The issues will not be reiterated here because most scientists accept the basic tenets of quantitative genetics. The focus of this book is on the use of this approach in the novel context of measures of the environment rather than measures of behavior.

Six other commentaries (Bradley and Caldwell, Duyme and Capron, Graham, Hay, Socha, Wachs) did not explicitly accept or reject the target article's major conclusion. However, they implicitly accepted the conclusion despite reservations about interpretations and implications of these findings.

Considering the novelty of the conclusion, it was most surprising that 19 of the 30 commentaries explicitly accepted the conclusion that genetic factors contribute to measures of the environment. These included commentaries by behavioral geneticists Boomsma and Molenaar; Crusio; Goodman and Stevenson; Hewitt; Johnson; Kendler; McGue and colleagues Bouchard and Lykken; Rowe; Scarr; Schulsinger; Turkheimer and Gottesman; Waldman and Weinberg; and Willerman. Most notably, the commentaries that agree with the conclusion include behavioral scientists who are most well known for their environmental research: Bronfenbrenner, Caspi, Lytton, Rutter, Simonton, and Tellegen.

The present review indicates that new research continues to support the conclusion that genetic factors contribute to diverse measures of the environment. These research findings raise several questions for future research. Four obvious questions involve generalization to other populations, use of other measures, gender differences, and development. The major question about generalization is whether results similar to those that emerge from research based on middle-class U.S. and European samples will be found in other cultures or at the extremes of children's environments such as abusive families. Concerning measures, although a diverse set of environmental measures has been investigated in the research to date, available measures are not necessarily the best measures. Other measures might yield different results. Next to nothing is known as yet about gender differences or developmental changes in the contribution of genetics to measures of the environment.

However, a key programmatic direction for research, as pointed out in several commentaries to the 1991 BBS target article, is to investigate the processes by which genetic factors contribute to environmental measures. The next chapter broaches this topic by considering factors that mediate the genetic contribution to environmental measures.

# 4

## Nature-Nurture

### *Mediators of the Genetic Contribution to Measures of the Environment*

The two preceding chapters presented empirical support for the hypothesis that genetic factors contribute to measures that are widely used as measures of the environment. This chapter turns to one version of the "how" rather than "how much" question: How do ostensible measures of the environment come to show genetic effects? This chapter approaches the hyphen in the nature-nurture interface largely from an empirical perspective by reviewing research that investigates mediators of the genetic contribution to measures of the environment. It uses multivariate genetic approaches to analyze the covariance between environmental measures and behavioral measures. Such analyses also broach the important topic of genetic mediation between environmental measures and behavioral measures typically considered outcome measures in the sense that such behavioral measures have been assumed to be the consequence of environmental measures with which they are correlated. For example, in the previous chapter, evidence that genetic factors contribute to measures of social support was reviewed. If there is a genetic contribution to social support as well as to psychopathology, this raises the possibility that associations between social support and psychopathology might be mediated by genetic factors.

Research on genetic mediation between environmental and behavioral measures can be considered in the framework of the quantitative genetic concept of genotype-environment (GE) correlation, discussed in the following section. The next chapter builds on this discussion of GE correlation to construct a theory of the genetics of experience.

## Genotype-Environment Correlation

GE correlation literally refers to a correlation between the genetic and environmental influences that affect a particular trait. It describes the extent to which individuals, as a function of their genetic propensities, are exposed to environments that in turn affect various aspects of their development. Genetic and environmental effects are the latent or anonymous components of variance in the fundamental equation of quantitative genetics, $V_P = V_G + V_E$. It can be shown that GE correlation adds the quantity 2 Cov(GE) to the phenotypic variance (e.g., Plomin, DeFries, & Loehlin, 1977). In other words, if $G$ and $E$ are positively correlated, phenotypic variance is increased.

It may still be necessary to note that GE correlation is different from the misleading notion that genetic and environmental effects cannot be studied separately because they "interact." This is usually couched in the innocuous phrase "behavior requires both genes and environment." Of course, DNA in a vacuum will not produce behavior nor will an environment without DNA. In this obvious sense, it is true that behavior cannot occur unless there is an organism to behave and an environment in which to behave. But this is not relevant to quantitative genetic analysis, which investigates individual differences in a population. Genetic differences among individuals can be important regardless of environmental effects. Environmental differences can be important regardless of genetic effects. Genetic and environmental influences can also interact in the statistical sense of a conditional relationship. That is, the effects of the environment might depend on the particular genotype. Genotype-environment interaction also adds to the phenotypic variance, and methods are available to identify specific genotype-environment interactions (Plomin et al., 1977). Examples of genotype-environment interactions can be found in biology and medicine (Rutter & Pickles, 1991). However, statistical detection of such effects is difficult statistically (Wahlsten, 1990) and empirical attempts to find such interactions in the realm of behavior have so far yielded little success (Plomin & Hershberger, 1991).

Although genotype-environment interaction is an important and interesting topic, the point of the present section is that genetic and environmental factors can also correlate. The reason for focusing on GE correlation is that it can address the question of mediators of the genetic contribution to measures of the environment.

THREE TYPES OF GE CORRELATION

Three types of GE correlation have been described (Plomin et al., 1977), and these lead to research strategies for finding mediators of the genetic contribution to environmental measures. *Passive* GE correlation occurs because children share heredity as well as environmental influences with members of their family. They can thus passively inherit environments correlated with their genetic propensities. For example, if musical ability is heritable (and this is not known), musically gifted children are likely to have musically gifted parents who provide them with both genes and an environment conducive to the development of musical ability. *Reactive*, or evocative, GE correlation refers to experiences of the child that derive from reactions of other people to the child's genetic propensities. For example, musically talented children might be picked out at school and given special opportunities. *Active* GE correlation occurs when individuals select or create environments that are correlated with their genetic propensities.

For example, even if no one does anything about a child's musical talent, the child might gravitate toward musical environments. Selection and creation of environments have been dubbed niche picking and niche building, respectively (Scarr & McCartney, 1983). In summary, passive GE correlation requires interactions between genetically related individuals. Reactive GE correlation can be induced by anyone who reacts to children on the basis of their inherent proclivities. Active GE correlation can involve anybody or anything in the environment (see Table 4.1). It should be mentioned that GE correlation can be negative, even though examples of positive correlations, such as those mentioned above, come more readily to mind. For example, slow learners may be given special attention to boost their performance. Cattell (1973, 1982) suggested that negative GE correlation may be common for personality. For instance, using dominance as an example, Cattell quipped that "society likes to 'cut down' individuals naturally too dominant and to help the humble inherit the earth" (Cattell, 1973, p. 145). Cattell refers to such examples of negative reactive GE correlation as "coercion to the biosocial norm." A theory of control systems (Bell, 1979) is similar to Cattell's concept of coercion to the biosocial norm. Parents are hypothesized to have upper and lower limits for intensity and appropriateness of children's behavior. When children's behavior exceeds the limit, parents begin to damp down; when children fall below a limit, parents attempt to stimulate.

Passive and active GE correlations can also be negative. Emotionally labile parents who are easily angered may have children with a proclivity to be quick-tempered, and yet the parents are likely to assail expressions of anger in their children, creating a negative passive GE correlation. Negative active GE correlation sounds almost pathological because we would not expect individuals to seek environments that rub against the grain of their dispositions. However, it seems reasonable to suppose, for example, that emotionally unstable children might seek calm environments and stable friends to steady their psyches, thus producing negative GE correlations of the active variety.

**TABLE 4.1** Three Types of Genotype-Environment Correlation

| Type | Description | Source of Environmental Influence |
|------|-------------|-----------------------------------|
| Passive | Children receive genotypes correlated with their family environment | Parents and siblings |
| Reactive | Children are reacted to on the basis of their genetic propensities | Anybody |
| Active | Children seek or create environments conducive to the development of their genetic propensities | Anybody or anything |

SOURCE: Plomin, R., DeFries, J., & Loehlin, J. C. (1977). Genotype-environment interaction and correlation in the analysis of human behavior. *Psychological Bulletin, 84,* 309-322. Copyright 1977 by the American Psychological Association. Reprinted by permission of the publisher.

## METHODS TO IDENTIFY MEASURED GE CORRELATION

In quantitative genetics, it is difficult to separate variance due to GE correlation from genetic and environmental components of variance (Plomin et al., 1977). Two methods have been used that are limited to the detection of variance due to passive GE correlation (Loehlin & DeFries, 1987). One method is based on model-fitting analyses of parent-child correlations in adoptive and nonadoptive families. The other method, which is less powerful, compares variances for adopted and nonadopted children. Analyses using both methods found no evidence for passive GE correlation for personality in infancy and early childhood (Plomin & DeFries, 1985; Plomin, DeFries, & Fulker, 1988) and in later childhood and adolescence (Loehlin, 1992). For IQ, however, these methods suggest substantial passive GE correlation, on the order of .15 to .25 (Loehlin & DeFries, 1987). Fortunately, the present search for mediators of the genetic contribution to environmental measures does not rest on estimating the magnitude of the anonymous component of variance to be attributed to GE correlation. It is actually easier to identify specific GE correlations in the sense of finding specific measures of the environment that are correlated genetically with behavior. Even if the components-of-variance approach finds little overall passive GE correlation, it is possible that passive GE correlation is important for particular combinations of behavioral and environmental dimensions. Moreover, reactive and active GE correlation can be important even if passive GE correlation is not.

In this chapter, three general methods are described that can be employed in the search for measured mediators of the genetic contribution to environmental measures. These methods address different types of GE correlation. The first method is the most general. It is a multivariate genetic analysis of the relationship between an environmental measure and a correlated measure. In contrast to traditional univariate genetic analysis of the variance of a single measure, multivariate genetic analysis decomposes the covariance between two measures into genetic and environmental sources of covariance.

Multivariate genetic analysis is described later, followed by two empirical examples of the application of multivariate genetic analysis to the covariation between environmental measures and behavioral measures. The first example involves the relationship between the HOME and children's mental development scores on the Bayley test using the child-based sibling adoption design of the Colorado Adoption Project. Because the HOME is a measure of family environment, genetic links between the HOME and the Bayley could involve passive GE correlation. For example, a genetic correlation between the HOME and the Bayley might emerge because the HOME relates to parents' IQ as well as to children's IQ. In this way, children might passively inherit genes and environment that are correlated in their effect on cognitive development. GE correlation assessed using multivariate genetic analysis is not limited to the passive variety. Parents might respond to gene-based propensities of their children (reactive GE correlation) and children might use their parents to get what they want (active GE correlation). For example, parents (whether genetically related or unrelated to their children) might read more to a child who obviously enjoys it (reactive GE correlation). And brighter children (whether adopted or not) can ask their parents to read to them or to get books for them (active GE correlation).

The second example involves the relationship between parenting and parents' personality using the adult twin-adoption design of SATSA. Here, active GE correlation seems most obvious. Consider a genetic correlation between warmth of parenting and parents' sociability. Sociable parents may seek out and foster warm interactions with their children as they do with other people. Nonetheless, reactive and passive sources of GE correlation are also possible. Parental sociability and warmth of parenting may be linked because children (including adopted children) reciprocate the warmth they receive from their sociable parents (reactive GE correlation). If the link between parents' sociability and warmth of parenting is only observed in families whose members are genetically related, this would signal passive GE correlation, which depends on both shared heredity and environment.

In summary, multivariate genetic analysis permits detection of GE correlations of any variety. After discussing this method and its results, a second method will be described that only detects passive GE correlation. A third method focuses on reactive and active GE correlation. By comparing the results of these three methods, it is possible to gauge the relative importance of the different kinds of GE correlation. This begins to address the mechanisms by which genetic mediation of environmental measures occurs.

## Genetic Correlates Of Environmental Measures

It has been suggested that the future of research on the nature of nurture lies in two programmatic directions: the investigation of the antecedents and the consequences of genetic involvement in environmental measures (Plomin & Neiderhiser, 1992b). The question of *antecedents* considers genetically influenced characteristics of individuals that result in genetic involvement in measures of the environment. In other words, the term *antecedents* refers to the mechanisms or at least indices of the genetic contribution to environmental measures.

The question of *consequences* concerns the extent to which genetic influences mediate associations between environmental measures and outcome variables. That is, if genetic factors contribute to environmental measures as well as to outcome measures, this raises the possibility that associations between environmental measures and outcomes can be explained genetically. Genetic mediation of associations between environmental measures and outcomes is the most important implication of finding a genetic contribution to environmental measures. Such research will lead to consideration of genetic involvement in risk, prevention, and intervention (Rende & Plomin, 1992).

The present discussion, however, considers both antecedents and consequences in the more general category of correlates of environmental measures. It is difficult to know whether a particular behavioral trait is an antecedent or a consequence in the causal sense. All we really know is that some traits are correlates of environmental measures. For example, consider the relationship between life events and depression. Although it might seem self-evident that this association occurs because negative life events lead to depression, the reverse may be possible: Depression may lead to negative life events. What about longitudinal data in which life events at one time are correlated with depression at a later time? (Research of this type is described later.) Even in this case, it is difficult to exclude the possibility that depression or some precursor of or predisposition to it preceded the negative life events. An extreme example in the literature involves the association between socioeconomic status (SES) and health. Surely the direction of effects is from SES to health. Not necessarily: A controversial hypothesis in this field of research, known as *health selection*, postulates that health affects adults' SES (West, 1991). For this reason, at this early stage of research, it is safer to talk about *correlates* rather than *antecedents* or *consequences*.

One other definitional issue concerns the use of the word *mediators* in the title of this chapter. A contemporary issue in developmental research concerns the distinction between moderators and mediators (Baron & Kenny, 1986). In addition to investigating the direct association between, for example, parental affection and children's adjustment, the effects of other variables can also be examined. Moderator variables refer to interactions, in the statistical sense of conditional relationships. For example, parental affection might predict children's adjustment differently for boys and girls. In contrast, "mediators speak to how or why such effects occur" (Baron & Kenny, 1986, p. 1176), the processes by which parental affection is associated with children's adjustment. In practice, mediators refer to other factors added in multivariate analyses. For example, children's self-esteem could be considered as a possible mediator of the relationships between parental affection and children's adjustment. Russell and Russell (1992) provide a discussion of moderators and mediators employing such socialization examples.

The concepts in this book do not fall neatly into this scheme of moderators and mediators, in part because genetic and environmental components of variance are inferred (latent) variables rather than measured variables. The basic finding of a genetic contribution to environmental measures was shown via inferred genetic and environmental components of variance. The word *mediation* is being used to refer to covariation between genetic effects on environmental measures and genetic effects on behavioral measures. For example, if a measure of parental affection shows a genetic contribution, to what extent can we account for that genetic contribution by shared genetic effects on behavioral measures? Genetics could be considered as a moderator if genotype- environment interactions were the analytic target (Rowe & Waldman, 1993). For example, heritability of children's adjustment might differ as a function of parental affection. This chapter examines the extent to which associations between environmental measures and behavioral measures are mediated genetically (Waldman & Weinberg, 1991). Clearly we are not studying moderators in the sense of interactions. Here, *mediation* is the better word, even though it is being used in a different context from the moderator-mediator distinction in developmental research.

The most obvious candidates for mediators of a genetic contribution to environmental measures are psychological traits. For example, genetic effects on the HOME might be due to genetic effects on intelligence of parents or intelligence of their children. Another possibility is that parenting might reflect parental personality. The genetic contribution to life events might be due to genetic effects on personality or psychopathology. There is no theory to guide the search for traits that mediate the genetic contribution to a particular environmental measure. One criterion is that candidate mediators must show heritability. However, this does not help much because most traits show moderate heritability. A reasonable first step is to investigate major traits such as intelligence, the personality "superfactors" of extraversion and neuroticism, and common psychopathological dimensions such as depression.

## Multivariate Genetic Analysis: Passive, Reactive, and Active GE Correlation

In order to explain genetic influences on environmental measures, it is not enough to show that measures of the environment are correlated phenotypically with measures of intelligence, personality, or psychopathology. Such correlations may arise for environmental reasons. That is, a phenotypic correlation between psychological traits and environmental measures cannot be assumed to be mediated genetically even when both the environmental and behavioral measures are heritable. For example, parenting may be correlated with parental personality for environmental rather than genetic reasons. Identifying genetic correlates of environmental measures requires multivariate genetic analysis. This section describes multivariate genetic analysis and presents two recent applications of this approach that attempt to identify genetic correlates of environmental measures.

### MULTIVARIATE GENETIC ANALYSIS

The gist of multivariate genetic analysis is the analysis of genetic and environmental contributions to the covariance between two measures rather than to the variance of each measure considered separately (Plomin & DeFries, 1979). Sophisticated model-fitting approaches to multivariate genetic analysis have been developed (Boomsma & Molenaar, 1986; Fulker, Baker, & Bock, 1983; Martin & Eaves, 1977; Neale & Cardon, 1992). These approaches have primarily been used to investigate the etiology of associations between measures in the same domain, most notably, to the analysis of cognitive abilities (e.g., Cardon & Fulker, 1993). The other major application of multivariate genetic analysis is to analyze longitudinal data, that is, covariance across time (e.g., Eaves, Hewitt, & Heath, 1988; Loehlin, Horn, & Willerman, 1989; Plomin & DeFries, 1981).

The Genetic Contribution to a Phenotypic Correlation Between a Measure of the Environment and a Behavioral Measure. The power of multivariate genetic analysis can be harnessed to study the etiology of associations between environmental measures and their correlates. Figure 4.1 is a path diagram that illustrates a bivariate genetic analysis between a measure of the environment and a correlate such as a measure of personality. The bivariate analysis decomposes genetic effects on the environmental measure into two components. One component (the latent variable G in Figure 4.1) represents genetic effects on the environmental measure that overlap with genetic effects on the correlate measure. The other component (the latent variable g in the figure) represents residual genetic effects on the environmental measure that are not shared with the correlate measure. In other words, the path from G to the environmental measure indicates genetic effects on the environmental measure that are shared in common with genetic effects on the other measure. The residual latent variable g represents the extent to which genetic effects on the environmental measure are independent of genetic effects on the other measure. Similarly, E and e are latent variables that represent common and unique environmental influences, respectively. Because the focus of this discussion is on the genetic contribution to environmental measures, these latent environmental variables are not shown as sub-

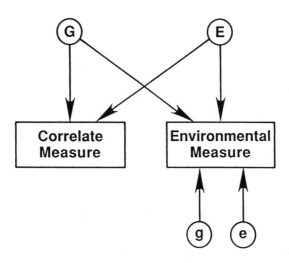

**Figure 4.1.** A bivariate genetic analysis of the extent to which genetic effects on an environmental measure can be explained by genetic effects on a correlate measure. See text for explanation of symbols.

divided into components representing shared and nonshared environment, as is usually done in such analyses.

Figure 4.1 indicates that the phenotypic correlation can be decomposed into its genetic and environmental contributions. The genetic contribution to the phenotypic correlation is estimated by the product of the paths that connect the two measures through G. The environmental contribution is estimated by the product of the paths that connect the two measures through E. Examples are provided later. The point to be made now is that genetic effects on an environmental measure are unlikely to be accounted for by another measure unless there is a phenotypic correlation between the two measures. That is, if two measures are uncorrelated, it makes little sense to decompose their correlation into genetic and environmental components. The only exception is that the G and E links could be of different signs, so that positive covariance of one cancels out negative covariance of the other, resulting in negligible phenotypic covariance. However, there are no examples of this occurring in multivariate genetic analyses. Thus, if there is no phenotypic correlation between an environmental measure and a behavioral measure, there is unlikely to be genetic links between them. For this reason, multivariate genetic analyses of the phenotypic association between environmental and behavioral measures must begin with a search for such associations.

Moreover, strong associations provide greater power for disentangling genetic and environmental sources of covariance. That is, if the correlation between an environmental measure and a behavioral measure is weak, there is little covariance to decompose and it is more difficult to do it. A provocative practical point along these lines is that, although environmental measures relate to many behavioral measures, the magnitude of the relationships is often small. This makes it unlikely that these behavioral variables will explain much of the genetic variance on environmental measures. For example, in the SATSA analysis of retrospective reports of childhood rearing environments (Plomin, McClearn, Pederson, Nesselroade, & Bergeman, 1988), associations with numerous dimensions of personality were examined. However, these associations were so weak that conducting multivariate genetic analyses seemed fruitless.

*The Genetic Correlation.* An exception to this conclusion lies in an additional concept concerning genetic mediation. The path diagram in Figure 4.1 is the standard way in which multivariate genetic analyses are presented and performed. An alternative presentation of the same model, shown in Figure 4.2, is helpful conceptually (e.g., Falconer, 1981; Plomin & DeFries, 1979). This model shows more clearly how multivariate genetic analysis is an extension of traditional univariate analysis. Multivariate genetic analysis goes beyond the analysis of variance of each trait to investigate the covariance between traits. As shown in Figure 4.2, a univariate genetic analysis can be applied to one measure, decomposing its variance into genetic and environmental components. (The paths $h_1$ and $h_2$ are the square roots of heritability, the

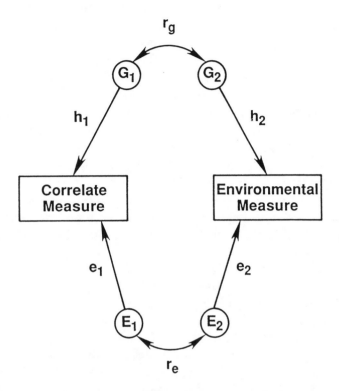

**Figure 4.2.** An alternative presentation of the path diagram in Figure 4.1; $r_g$ is the genetic correlation between genetic effects on the two measures ($G_1$ and $G_2$). $r_e$ is the environmental correlation between environmental effects on the two measures ($E_1$ and $E_2$).

proportion of phenotypic variance attributed to genetic variance.) The other measure can be analyzed similarly.

The novel concept of multivariate genetic analysis is the genetic correlation ($r_g$), indicated by the double-headed arrow connecting G for the two measures. The genetic correlation is the correlation between genetic influences that affect one measure and genetic influences that affect the other measure. If genetic effects on the two measures do not overlap, the genetic correlation is zero. If genetic effects on one measure completely covary with genetic effects on the other, the genetic correlation is 1.0. Figure 4.2 indicates that the genetic contribution to the phenotypic correlation between the two measures is the product of the chain of paths, $h_1 \times r_g \times h_2$. This is equivalent to the product of the two paths from $G$ in Figure 4.1. As discussed in relation to Figure 4.1, the path from $G$ to the environmental measure indicates genetic effects on the environmental measure that are shared in common with genetic effects on the other measure. This path is equivalent to $h_2 \times r_g$, not $r_g$ itself, assuming that $G$ in Figure 4.1 is equivalent to $G_1$ in Figure 4.2. In other words, the path from $G$ to the environmental measure in Figure 4.1 includes portions of both the genetic correlation and heritability of the environmental measure.

Conceptually, it is useful to disentangle these two factors. Heritabilities of two measures can be low, but their genetic correlation can be high. This indicates that, although genetic effects do not account for much of the variance for one or both of the measures, what genetic effects exist are substantially shared. As we shall see, this case applies to some analyses of associations between environmental measures and their correlates. Conversely, heritability can be high but the genetic correlation can be low. This indicates that, although genetic effects substantially account for phenotypic variance of both measures, genetic effects do not overlap.

In this sense, the genetic correlation refers to the nature of the genetic relationship between the two measures regardless of the strength of their genetic effects on the phenotypic measures. The genetic correlation ($r_g$) answers some questions and the genetic chain of paths ($h_1 \times r_g \times h_2$) answers others. The latter indicates the extent to which the phenotypic correlation between an environmental measure and another measure is mediated genetically. To repeat, $h_1 \times r_g \times h_2$ is the genetic correlation weighted by the square roots of the heritabilities for the two measures, which has the effect of standardizing the genetic covariance in terms of its contribution to the phenotypic variance (for details, see Plomin & DeFries, 1979). The genetic correlation, on the other hand, indicates the extent to which genetic effects overlap for the two measures regardless of their relative contribution to phenotypic variance. In sum, these two different ways of looking at the same data can paint different pictures concerning the extent of overlap between genetic effects on an environmental measure and another measure. For this reason, both are considered below.

*Estimation.* How do we estimate the genetic contribution to the phenotypic correlation? Using the twin method as an example, instead of correlating one twin's score with the twin partner's score on the same variable, cross-twin correlations are analyzed. A cross-twin correlation is the correlation between one twin's score on one measure and the other twin's score on the other measure. Everything else is similar to the usual univariate analysis of a single measure. In univariate analysis, doubling the difference between MZ and DZ twin correlations estimates heritability ($h^2$), the proportion of phenotypic variance attributed to genetic variance. In bivariate analysis, doubling the difference between MZ and DZ cross-twin correlations estimates the genetic contribution to the phenotypic correlation ($h_1 \times r_g \times h_2$). In univariate analysis, phenotypic variance is the sum of genetic variance and environmental variance; in bivariate analysis, the phenotypic correlation is the sum of its genetic and environmental contributions. How do we disentangle the genetic correlation from the genetic chain of paths? If we know the genetic chain of paths, $h_1 \times r_g \times h_2$ and we know the heritabilities ($h_1$ and $h_2$), then $r_g$ can be estimated as $h_1 \times r_g \times h_2$ divided by $h_1 \times h_2$ (for details, see Plomin & DeFries, 1979).

In practice, multivariate genetic analysis is conducted using model-fitting analyses of the model represented in Figure 4.1 (Martin & Eaves, 1977; Neale & Cardon, 1992). Genetic covariance between two measures is estimated as the product of the paths that connect the two measures through G. The genetic correlation is estimated as the genetic covariance divided by the genetic variance.

HOME, IQ, AND TEMPERAMENT

As discussed in Chapter 2, the HOME, an observational/interview measure of the home environment relevant to cognitive development, shows substantial genetic effects at both 1 and 2 years of age (Braungart et al., 1992). Employing the sibling adoption design that compares adoptive and nonadoptive siblings, substantial heritability was also found at 1 and 2 years for the Bayley Mental Development Index. To what extent do genetic effects on the HOME overlap with genetic effects on the Bayley?

Multivariate genetic analysis was conducted using the sibling adoption design that employs nonadoptive and adoptive cross-sibling correlations, that is, correlating one sibling's HOME score with the other sibling's Bayley score. If genetic effects on the HOME covary with genetic effects on the Bayley, nonadoptive cross-sibling correlations will exceed those for adoptive siblings. At 1 year of age, the nonadoptive and adoptive cross-sibling correlations are .13 and .17, respectively. This pattern of results suggests no genetic overlap between the HOME and the Bayley at 1 year. However, at 2, the cross-sibling correlations are .37 and .12, respectively, indicating genetic overlap.

A multivariate genetic analysis treats these issues more rigorously and elegantly, with the results illustrated in the path diagram in Figure 4.3. Path diagrams are useful in presenting such results because the contribution of the latent variables to the measured variables is indicated by the square of the paths, which are standardized partial regression coefficients. That is, the variance of the HOME is accounted for by the sum of the squares of the six paths leading to the HOME, assuming that the latent variables are uncorrelated. [Unlike Figure 4.1, the environmental component of variance in Figure 4.3 is subdivided into shared (Es) and nonshared (En) environment.] For example, for year 1 results in the top portion of Figure 4.3, $.03^2 + .56^2 + .13^2 + .74^2 + .00^2 + .42^2 = 1.0$.

Genetic variance on the HOME is decomposed into two components. The path from G represents the extent to which genetic effects on the HOME measure covary with genetic effects on the Bayley. The path from the residual $g$ latent variable indicates the extent to which genetic variance on the HOME does not overlap with genetic effects on the Bayley. At 1 year, it can be seen that the G path is only .03, whereas the $g$ path is .74. This means that genetic effects on the HOME do not overlap with genetic effects on the 1-year-old Bayley. As mentioned earlier, the product of the

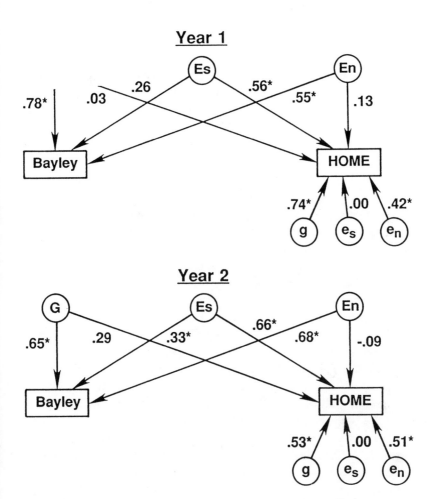

**Figure 4.3.** A bivariate analysis of the extent to which genetic effects on the HOME can be explained by genetic effects on the Bayley Mental Development Index at 1 and 2 years (Braungart, Fulker, & Plomin, 1992). See text concerning Figure 4.1 for explanation of symbols.

SOURCE: Braungart, J. M., Fulker, D. W., & Plomin, R. (1992). Genetic influence of the home environment during infancy: A sibling adoption study of the HOME. *Developmental Psychology, 28*, 1048-1055. Copyright 1992 by the American Psychological Association. Reprinted by permission of the publisher.

paths from G to the Bayley and to the HOME estimates the genetic contribution to the phenotypic correlation between the two measures. This estimate is negligible (.78 × .03 = .02). The lack of genetic covariance between the HOME and the 1-year-old Bayley is reflected in a weak phenotypic association between the two variables at 1 year. At 1 year, the phenotypic correlation is typically about .20; the correlation is nearly twice as great at 2 years (Bradley et al., 1989; Gottfried & Gottfried, 1984).

At 2 years, some genetic overlap between the HOME and Bayley can be seen. The path from G is .29 and the path from $g$ is .53. Although the path from G is not significant, the results suggest that almost a quarter of the genetic variance on the HOME can be accounted for by genetic effects on the Bayley [that is, $.29^2 \div (.29^2 + .53^2) = .23$]. This same result implies that three quarters of the genetic variance on the HOME cannot be accounted for by genetic effects on the Bayley. Nonetheless, Figure 4.3 indicates that genetic factors contribute substantially to the phenotypic correlation between the HOME and the Bayley at 2 years. The phenotypic correlation can be estimated from Figure 4.3 as .35 [i.e., $(.65 \times .29) + (.33 \times .66) + (.68 \times -.09) = .35$], which is the same as the actual correlation between the HOME and the Bayley calculated from these data. The genetic contribution is about .20 (i.e., $.65 \times .29 = .19$). In other words, genetic factors are estimated to account for more than half of the phenotypic association between the HOME and the Bayley (i.e., $.19 \div .35 = .54$).

As discussed in the previous section, although the path from G indicates that genetic effects on the HOME covary with genetic effects on the Bayley, it conflates heritability and the genetic correlation (i.e., $h_2 \times r_g$). Heritability of the HOME is the sum of the squared paths to the HOME from G and $g$. Dividing the path from G ($h_2 \times r_g$) by $h_2$ estimates the genetic correlation, where $h_2$ is the square root of heritability of the HOME.

At 1 year, the path from G ($h_2 \times r_g$) is .03. The heritability of the HOME is .55 (i.e., $.03^2 + .74^2$). Thus, the genetic correlation is negligible, .04 (i.e., $.03 \div \sqrt{.55}$). Both the path from G and the genetic correlation suggests that the genetic effects on the HOME at 1 are not at all accounted for by genetic effects on the Bayley.

At year 2, the genetic correlation suggests somewhat greater genetic overlap between the HOME and the Bayley than does the path from $G$; $h_2 \times r_g$ is .29, and the heritability of the HOME is .37 (i.e., $.29^2 + .53^2$). Thus, the genetic correlation is .48 (i.e., $.29 + \sqrt{.37}$). Although only a quarter of the genetic variance on the HOME can be accounted for by genetic effects on the Bayley, the genetic correlation indicates that, setting aside their heritabilities, about half of their genetic effects covary. Nonetheless, this genetic correlation implies that about half of their genetic effects do not covary.

As indicated in Chapter 1, the version of the HOME used in the Colorado Adoption Project shows little heritability in early childhood at 3 and 4 years of age. It also shows meager phenotypic relationships with IQ in early childhood. Thus, it makes no sense to ask whether IQ mediates genetic effects on the HOME in early childhood because there are no genetic effects on the HOME at that age and because their phenotypic correlation is so low. However, it is interesting that the HOME at 1 and 2 predicts Stanford-Binet IQ at 3 and 4 and that this relationship is mediated genetically (Plomin, DeFries, & Fulker, 1988). For example, the longitudinal cross-sibling correlation between the HOME at 1 year and IQ at 4 years is .24 for nonadoptive siblings and –.02 for adoptive siblings. This finding makes the point that longitudinal relationships between environmental measures and later assessed behavioral correlates cannot be assumed to be mediated environmentally.

Of course, genetic effects on characteristics of children other than intelligence might also overlap with genetic effects on the HOME. Cognitive factors not assessed by the Bayley is one possibility. Temperament is another possibility, although reviews of nongenetic studies of parenting and child temperament find inconsistent associations (Crockenberg, 1986; Slabach, Morrow, & Wachs, 1991). The lack of strong phenotypic associations between parenting and child temperament makes it less likely that children's temperament mediates genetic effects on measures of parenting. Nonetheless, a multivariate genetic analysis of tester ratings on the Bayley Infant Behavior Record (IBR) as they relate to the HOME yielded an interesting result (Braungart, in press). Task Orientation is one of three factors that emerge from factor analyses of the IBR items rated by the tester during administration of the Bayley mental test (Matheny, 1980). This factor consists of three items: responsiveness to objects, attention span, and goal directedness. In model-fitting analyses in which both the HOME and Task Orientation were averaged at 1 and 2, Task Orientation was found to explain all of the genetic variance on the HOME. Although it makes sense that parents' scores on the HOME might reflect genetically influenced attentional characteristics of their infants, caution is warranted until this result is replicated.

If Task Orientation does not in fact completely explain genetic effects on the HOME, other candidates include genetically influenced characteristics of parents such as intelligence and personality. Such parental characteristics would be especially good candidates if passive GE correlation were responsible for genetic effects on the HOME. This is discussed in the following section.

It is also possible that genetic contributions to the HOME will not be accounted for entirely by traditional traits of children or of parents. Although these are very early days in research on the mediators of genetic effects on environmental measures, this seems to be the picture that is emerging. Some genetic effects on environmental measures can be accounted for by genetic effects on trait measures, but most cannot.

PARENTING AND PERSONALITY

Determinants of individual differences in parenting have received relatively little attention compared to the huge research literature on the effects of parenting on children's development. A review of the correlates of parenting emphasizes the importance of parental personality, life events, and social support (Belsky, 1984). Genetic influence on these domains and thus on their relationship with parenting has not been mentioned in this literature.

In Chapter 2, SATSA research was reviewed that showed a genetic contribution to perceptions of current family environment as assessed by the FES using a parent-based genetic design (Plomin et al., 1989). To what extent are genetic effects on the FES due to parents' personality? A recent report examined possible genetic mediation of the FES by the two "superfactors" of personality, and neuroticism and extraversion (Chipuer, Plomin, Pedersen, McClearn, & Nesselroade, 1992). Neuroticism and extraversion are two of the most pervasive and most highly heritable personality factors in SATSA (Pedersen, Plomin, McClearn, & Friberg, 1988) and in reviews of other research (e.g., Eaves et al., 1989; Loehlin, 1992a).

The bivariate design described in relation to Figure 4.1 was extended to the trivariate case (see Figure 4.4) in order to investigate the extent to which genetic effects on neuroticism and extraversion in concert account for genetic effects on the FES. In these analyses, the second-order FES factors were employed: Relationship (cohesion, conflict, expressiveness), Personal Growth (culture, recreation, achievement orientation), and System Maintenance (control, organization), rather than the primary factors used in the original report of univariate analyses of the FES (Plomin et al., 1989). Heritability is about 30% for each of the three second-order FES factors.

The results indicate that genetic effects on extraversion and neuroticism contribute to genetic effects on the FES. However, most genetic effects on the environmental measures are independent of genetic effects on these two major dimensions of personality. Figure 4.4 depicts the results in path analytic form for the Relationship factor. (In order to simplify the presentation, only the genetic paths are included in Figure 4.4.) The trivariate model decomposes the variance of neuroticism, extraversion, and the FES environmental measure into genetic variance that is common to all three variables ($G_1$), genetic variance independent of $G_1$ but common to Extraversion and the FES measure ($G_2$), and genetic variance that is unique to the environmental measure ($g$).

As discussed in relation to Figure 4.3, summing the squared path coefficients leading to the Relationship factor indicates that the heritability of this environmental measure is about 30% (i.e., $-.19^2 + .17^2 + .49^2 = .30$). Genetic effects on the Relationship factor that are independent of Neuroticism and Extraversion are indicated by the path from the residual latent variable, $g$. Thus, the proportion of genetic variance unique to the Relationship factor is about 80% [i.e., $.49^2 \div (-.19^2 + .17^2 + .49^2) = .79$].

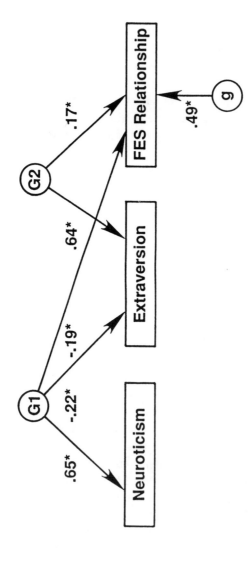

**Figure 4.4.** A trivariate analysis of the extent to which genetic effects on the FES Relationship factor can be explained by genetic effects on Neuroticism and Extraversion. Only genetic latent variables are shown. See text concerning Figure 4.1 for explanation of symbols.

SOURCE: Chipuer, H. M., Plomin, R., Pedersen, N. L., McClearn, G. E., & Nesselroade, J. R. (1992). Genetic influence on family environment: The role of personality. *Developmental Psychology, 29*, 110-118. Copyright 1992 by the American Psychological Association. Reprinted by permission of the publisher.

Finding that 80% of the genetic variance of the Relationship factor is unique implies that 20% of the genetic variance of the FES Relationship factor can be accounted for by these personality traits. This can be derived directly in Figure 4.4 as the sum of the squared G paths to the FES measure ($-.19^2 + .17^2 = .06$) divided by the heritability of the FES measure ($.06 \div .30 = .20$). The paths from G are significant, which indicates that genetic variance on the FES measure is significantly mediated by the personality measures.

Another question that can be addressed by multivariate genetic analysis is the extent to which genetic influences contribute to the phenotypic correlation between the measures. The phenotypic correlation between Neuroticism and FES Relationship is $-.16$. The genetic contribution to this phenotypic correlation is the product of the G paths connecting them ($.65 \times -.19 = -.12$). In other words, about 75% of the phenotypic correlation is contributed by genetics (i.e., $-.12 \div -.16 = .75$). The phenotypic correlation between Extraversion and FES Relationship is $.16$ and the genetic contribution is $.15$ [$(-.22 \times -.19 = .04) + (.64 \times .17 = .11) = .15$]. Thus, nearly all of the phenotypic correlation is mediated genetically.

There is no contradiction in the finding that most of the genetic variance of the FES measures is not accounted for by the personality measures and the finding that genetic influences account for most of the phenotypic correlation between the FES measures and personality. The reason is the modest phenotypic correlation between the FES measures and personality. Similarly modest phenotypic correlations have been found between adult children's ratings of their own personality and their ratings of their parents' behavior (McCrae & Costa, 1988).

As in the previous example of genetic overlap between the HOME and the Bayley, the genetic correlations between the FES and the personality measures suggest somewhat greater overlap in the nature of their genetic effects, setting aside the strength of their effects on the phenotype. In the trivariate model, the same principles apply for calculating the genetic correlation but the calculation is made more difficult by having three variables. The genetic correlation can be calculated by using the genetic contribution to the phenotypic correlation, which as shown above is $-.12$

for Neuroticism. This represents $h_1 \times h_3 \times r_g$, where $h_1$ is the square root of the heritability of Neuroticism and $h_3$ is the square root of the heritability of the FES measure. Dividing this product (−.12) by the product of $h_1 \times h_3$ (i.e., .65 × .55 = .36) estimates $r_g$ as −.33 (−.12 ÷ .36 = −.33). The genetic correlation is .40 between Extraversion and this FES measure.

Results for the FES Personal Growth factor are nearly identical. Although genetic effects on Neuroticism and Extraversion significantly covary with genetic effects on this FES factor, 79% of the genetic variance on the FES Personal Growth factor is unique. The genetic correlation is −.29 with Neuroticism and −.42 with Extraversion.

For the FES System Maintenance factor, all of the genetic variance is independent of Neuroticism and Extraversion and the genetic correlations are also negligible. This occurs because the phenotypic correlations between the FES System Maintenance factor and Neuroticism and Extraversion are negligible ($r = .02$ and −.03, respectively). This latter finding may be important in that parental control again appears to be behaving differently than other aspects of parenting. That is, in child-based genetic designs, parental control shows lower heritability than other measures of parenting. In contrast, in parent-based designs such as SATSA, from which the present analyses are derived, the control factor shows heritability. However, the present findings indicate no genetic overlap with personality for this control measure, whereas genetic effects on the other dimensions of parenting are mediated at least in part by personality.

In summary, as in the previous example of the HOME and the Bayley measure of mental development, some genetic effects on the FES can be accounted for by genetic effects on personality, but the majority cannot. Two recent abstracts of work in progress support this conclusion. A study of parents who are twins or pairs of unrelated children reared together also suggests that some genetic effects on parenting are shared with the "big five" dimensions of personality, which include neuroticism and extraversion (Rowe et al., 1992). The child-based genetic design of the NEAD project discussed in Chapters 2 and 3 also indicates that some genetic variance on child and parent reports of family environment can be explained by genetic effects on personality, psychopathology, and perceived self-competence (McGuire, Reiss, Hetherington, & Plomin, 1992). However, genetic effects on most measures of family environment are largely independent of these other variables.

OTHER MULTIVARIATE GENETIC ANALYSES

Other relevant multivariate genetic research on this topic will be mentioned more briefly. These research reports include attempts to identify genetic correlates of environmental measures, such as family environment, social support, life events, SES, and television viewing.

*Family Environment and Temperament in Middle Childhood.* A Colorado Adoption Project analysis mentioned earlier suggested that tester ratings on the Infant Behavior Record (IBR) scale of Task Orientation might substantially account for genetic effects on the HOME in infancy (Braungart, in press). This is the only case in which the genetic contribution to an environmental measure (the HOME) can be accounted for in its entirety by a behavioral measure (IBR Task Orientation). However, as discussed earlier, this result needs to be replicated before it is taken too seriously.

This report (Braungart, in press) was also mentioned in Chapter 2 because it found that parents' ratings of their parenting warmth and consistency showed genetic effects when their children were 7 and 9 years old. Multivariate genetic analysis revealed that tester ratings of the children's temperament in infancy and early childhood, including IBR Task Orientation, did not contribute to these genetic effects on self-reported parenting in middle childhood.

*Social Support, Depression, and Life Satisfaction.* As discussed in Chapter 3, a measure of perceived adequacy of social support showed genetic effects in SATSA analyses (Bergeman et al., 1990). In SATSA, the strongest phenotypic correlates of social support are depression and life satisfaction, even though these phenotypic correlations are only about .20. Interpretations of these correlations typically assume that social support decreases depression and increases life satisfaction. However, SATSA analyses indicate genetic effects for both depression and life satisfaction, which raises the possibility that their associations with social support may be mediated genetically. The answer again is that genetic effects on these traits can account for some, but not all, genetic effects on social support (Bergeman, Plomin, Pedersen, & McClearn, 1991).

Another twin study described in Chapter 3 also found evidence for a genetic contribution to social support (Kessler et al., 1992). A multivariate genetic analysis of social support and depressed mood confirmed the SATSA finding of genetic mediation. An interesting analysis examined the interaction between social support and life events in predicting depressed mood. As typically found in social support research, the association between social support and adjustment is stronger under greater stress (Thoits, 1986). Multivariate genetic analysis suggested that this interaction is due in part to genetic factors. The authors hypothesized that stressful life events might engage genetic effects on social support that are shared to a greater extent with genetic effects on depressed mood.

Of course, these results do not imply that all or even most of the association between social support and adjustment is mediated genetically. For example, an environmental contribution to the association between social support and depression is suggested by research showing that experimentally induced depression results in lower ratings of social support (Cohen, Towbes, & Flocco, 1988). As in any experiment, it cannot be presumed that this result reflects the processes that affect the association outside the laboratory. The best evidence for the importance of nongenetic mediation comes from multivariate genetic analysis: Phenotypic associations between environmental measures such as social support and behavioral measures such as depressed mood can only be explained in part by genetic mediation. This conclusion applies as well to the following examples of multivariate genetic analysis.

*Life Events and Personality.* A SATSA analysis suggesting a genetic contribution to life events was also discussed in Chapter 3

(Plomin, Lichtenstein, et al., 1990). What are the genetic correlates of life events such as conflicts, financial disruption, accident, and illnesses? For example, neuroticism has been shown to relate to life events (Brett, Brief, Burke, George, & Webster, 1990). More specifically, conflicts might be induced by genetic effects on the anger component of emotionality. IQ might contribute to financial problems. Risk-taking might be involved in accidents, and illness might be affected by genetic factors involved in susceptibility to disease.

Although these possibilities have not yet been thoroughly explored, depression correlates phenotypically with life events in SATSA and this association has been subjected to a multivariate genetic analysis (Neiderhiser, Plomin, Lichtenstein, Pedersen, & McClearn, 1992). The results indicate that genetic effects on life events and depression overlap. This genetic association between life events and depression remains when depression was assessed 3 years later and again 6 years later. However, as mentioned earlier, such longitudinal associations do not imply causality because genetic effects on depression 6 years after the initial assessment overlap substantially with genetic effects on depression at the initial assessment.

*SES and IQ.* Multivariate genetic analyses also indicate that IQ can account for some genetic effects on SES in adulthood (Lichtenstein et al., 1992; Tambs et al., 1989). About half of the genetic effects on SES are independent of IQ, however.

*SES and Health.* SES and health both show heritability and the association between them has been shown to be in part genetically mediated (Lichtenstein, Harris, Pedersen, & McClearn, in press).

*Television Viewing.* As indicated in Chapter 2, individual differences in children's television viewing show strong genetic effects. Can this be explained by intelligence or temperament? Neither intelligence nor temperament of children appears to be responsible for this genetic contribution (Plomin, Corley et al., 1990). For example, the correlation between IQ and television was −.01 at 3 years and .01 at 4 years. The range of correlations for temperament measures was only −.08 to .08. Because television viewing showed no phenotypic correlations with these behavioral variables, multivariate genetic analyses were not undertaken.

## Environment-Behavior Correlations in Nonadoptive Versus Adoptive Homes: Passive GE Correlation

To recap, research reviewed in Chapters 2 and 3 indicated that genetic factors play a role in many environmental measures. The goal of this chapter is to consider mechanisms by which that happens. Multivariate genetic analysis, discussed in the previous section, addresses this issue, capturing genetic mediation due to GE correlation of any kind. This section and the next attempt to go one step farther by exploring the extent to which this genetic mediation is due specifically to passive GE correlation or to reactive and active GE correlation.

A different design used to investigate genetic mediation of associations between environmental measures and behavioral measures focuses on genetic mediation that arises from passive GE correlation (Plomin, Loehlin, & DeFries, 1985). What if an association between a measure of family environment and children's behavior is greater in nonadoptive families than in adoptive families? For instance, what if the correlation between the HOME and scores on the Bayley is greater in nonadoptive families than in adoptive families? The general answer is that genetic factors mediate the HOME-Bayley correlation. The specific answer is that passive GE correlation is responsible, assuming that variances are similar in nonadoptive and adoptive families.

This design pinpoints passive GE correlation because HOME-Bayley correlations in nonadoptive and adoptive families would not be expected to differ if reactive or active GE correlation were at work. Adoptive children have genes too, and parents respond to gene-based differences in adopted children (reactive GE correlation). Also, adopted children, like other children, get their way with their parents (active GE correlation). The difference is that adopted children share environment but not genes with their parents and thus miss out on passive GE correlation. Two benefits of this design are that it requires only singleton adopted children, not siblings or parents, and that it is so simple and direct. It is difficult to think of a name for this design. It is like a parent-offspring design with the parental variables unspecified. As a default label, the approach can be referred to as the *measured passive GE correlation design*.

Figure 4.5 illustrates this design as a path diagram. The path diagram indicates that in nonadoptive families the correlation between the HOME and the Bayley can occur in two ways: either environmentally via the *fe* chain of paths or genetically via the parents' and child's genotypes, i.e., passive GE correlation. This latter path is $\frac{1}{2}rh$ for the path through each parent's unmeasured genotype $G$ with a combined value of $rh$ for the genetic paths, assuming that $r$ is equal for mothers and fathers. The residual arrows allow for other causes.

For adoptive families on the right of Figure 4.5, the HOME has only an environmental connection to the child's Bayley. The genotypes of the biological parents will not contribute to the correlation between the HOME and the child's Bayley in the absence of selective placement. This correlation then simply takes on the value *fe*.

In summary, the HOME-Bayley correlation is *fe* + *rh* in nonadoptive families and just *fe* in adoptive families. It follows that the difference between the correlations in nonadoptive and adoptive families estimates *rh*, the genetic contribution to the HOME-Bayley correlation. As mentioned earlier, correlations such as the HOME-Bayley correlation might also reflect reactive and active GE correlation in both nonadoptive and adoptive families, but these effects of reactive and active GE correlation would be cancelled out in the difference between the correlations in nonadoptive and adoptive families. This leaves passive GE correlation as the sole source of the difference.

This measured passive GE correlation design has been generalized to the multivariate analysis of several environmental and behavioral variables (Thompson, Fulker, DeFries, & Plomin, 1986).

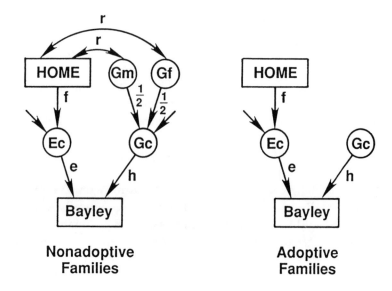

**Figure 4.5.** An adoption design to detect passive GE correlation by comparing the correlation between the HOME and children's Bayley scores in nonadoptive and adoptive families. See text for explanation of symbols.

SOURCE: Plomin, R., Loehlin, J. C., & DeFries, J. C. (1985). Genetic and environmental components of "environmental" influences. *Developmental Psychology, 21,* 391-402. Copyright 1985 by the American Psychological Association. Reprinted by permission of the publisher.

It has also been combined with the usual parent-offspring adoption model in order to test the model more rigorously (Coon, Fulker, DeFries, & Plomin, 1990; Rice, Fulker, DeFries, & Plomin, 1988) and generalized to the multivariate case (Cherny, in press).

As in multivariate genetic analysis, the measured passive GE correlation method requires that a measure of the environment is correlated with a measure of development. That is, if an association does not exist, the genetic and environmental contributions to the association cannot be analyzed. Moreover, the magnitude of the association must at least be moderate. The issue is effect size rather than mere statistical significance. The most difficult part of this program of research is finding associations between environmental measures and measures of development that are of reasonable effect size (Maccoby & Martin, 1983), even though some environmentalists continue to assume the contrary (e.g., Hoffman, 1991; cf. Bouchard, in press).

For example, we attempted to apply this method to the association between linguistic environment and infant communicative development (Hardy-Brown & Plomin, 1985). The linguistic environments of children were laboriously scored from phonetic transcriptions of videotapes of mother-infant interaction in 50 adoptive and 50 nonadoptive families. Maternal speech characteristics included frequency of vocalization and communicative gesturing, sentence types, imitation of infant vocalizations, nonimitative contingent vocal responding, tuitional modeling of language, mean length of utterance, and self-repetition. However, these traditional measures of the linguistic environment showed only slightly more than a chance number of significant associations with children's communicative competence. Without reasonable phenotypic associations between linguistic environment and children's communicative competence, comparisons between adoptive and nonadoptive families were pointless.

Following are examples in which at least modest phenotypic associations between environmental measures and outcome measures could be detected, thus making it possible to apply the measured passive GE correlation method. The first example involves the association between the HOME and IQ.

HOME AND IQ

In the previous section, a multivariate genetic analysis of the HOME and the Bayley was presented using the sibling adoption design of the Colorado Adoption Project (Braungart et al., 1992). The results (Figure 4.3) indicated that genetic factors in common between the HOME and the Bayley account for about half of the phenotypic correlation between the HOME and the Bayley when the children were 2 years old. The design in Figure 4.5 can be used to investigate the extent to which this genetic mediation at 2 is due to passive GE correlation. Application of this design is limited to the Colorado Adoption Project because it is the only adoption study that includes measures of the environment other than parental education and socioeconomic status.

The results, shown in Table 4.2, are similar to those of the multivariate genetic analysis (Figure 4.3). Genetic mediation is suggested at age 2 but not at age 1. At 2 years, the phenotypic correlation between the HOME and Bayley is .42 in nonadoptive families and .27 in adoptive families. As discussed earlier, the genetic component ($rh$) to the HOME-Bayley correlation is estimated as .15 (i.e., .42 − .27 = .15) at age 2. Thus, genetic factors assessed by this design account for about a third (i.e., .15 ÷ .42 = .36) of the HOME-Bayley correlation at 2 years (Plomin, DeFries, & Fulker, 1988).

The point of this section is that genetic effects detected by this design are limited to passive GE correlation. In contrast, the multivariate genetic results discussed in relation to Figure 4.3 suggest that about half of the HOME-Bayley correlation at 2 years is due to genetic mediation. The multivariate genetic design detects active and reactive GE correlation in addition to passive GE correlation. Although all of these analyses require replication, together they suggest that passive GE correlation accounts for some but not all of the genetic mediation of the relationship between the HOME and Bayley.

Previous analyses in the Colorado Adoption Project suggested that these genetic links between the HOME and Bayley primarily involve a HOME factor called Encouraging Developmental Advance (Plomin et al., 1985). Correlations between this HOME factor and the Bayley at year 2 are .44 in nonadoptive families and .22 in adoptive families. These analyses also suggested some specificity in relation to mental development. Genetic mediation appeared to be strongest for Verbal (symbolic) and Lexical factors derived from the Bayley items. Buttressing this conclusion is the finding that the HOME also shows strong genetic links with the Sequenced Inventory of Communication Development (SICD). The correlations between the HOME and the SICD are .50 in nonadoptive families and .32 in adoptive families.

The Colorado Adoption Project version of the HOME in early childhood at 3 and 4 years shows little effect of genetics, as indicated in Chapter 2. Thus there is no reason to examine medi-

**TABLE 4.2** Passive GE Correlation: HOME-Bayley Correlations for Non-adopted and Adopted Infants at Ages 1 and 2

|  | HOME-Bayley Correlations | |
| Age | Nonadoptive Families | Adoptive Families |
|---|---|---|
| 1 Year | .05 | .12 |
| 2 Years | .42 | .27 |

SOURCE: Adapted from Plomin, DeFries, & Fulker (1988).
NOTE: N = 241 adopted and 245 nonadopted probands at 1 and 212 adopted and 229 nonadopted at 2.

ators of genetic effects on the HOME at this age. Correlations with Stanford-Binet IQ scores are .15 for nonadopted children and .11 for adopted children at 3 years and .16 and .10, respectively, at 4 years (Plomin, DeFries, & Fulker, 1988). This suggests at most a modest role for passive GE correlation in early childhood for these measures. However, as mentioned in regards to multivariate analyses of longitudinal relationships, the HOME at 1 year shows genetic links to IQ at 3 and 4 years. Longitudinal correlations between the HOME and children's IQ in nonadoptive and adoptive families indicate that these genetic links involve passive GE correlation. Correlations between the HOME at 1 year and IQ at 3 years are .15 in nonadoptive and .08 in adoptive families; at 4 years, the correlations are .16 and .06, respectively (Plomin, DeFries, & Fulker, 1988).

Surprisingly, the HOME in infancy predicts IQ in middle childhood slightly more strongly than in early childhood (Coon et al., 1990). The HOME at year 1 correlates with WISC-R IQ at 7 years .21 in nonadoptive and −.08 in adoptive families. Correlations for the HOME at year 2 are .31 and .08, respectively. Thus these results suggest that to the extent that the HOME relates to children's IQ, it does so primarily for reasons of passive GE correlation. This report also showed that, at 7 years, several scales of the FES correlate with children's IQ primarily for genetic reasons. These results have been extended to 9 years of age (Cherny, in press).

It is interesting that in the Colorado Adoption Project parental education and SES yield results similar to those for the HOME. Multiple correlations predicting offspring IQ from parental education and occupational status for nonadoptive and adoptive children are .20 and .16, respectively, at 1 year, .23 and .05 at 2 years, .22 and .19 at 3 years, and .16 and .12 at 4 years. The significant difference in correlations at 2, the lower correlations at 3 and 4, and the lack of evidence for genetic mediation other than at 2 support the results that emerged for the HOME.

These results from the Colorado Adoption Project led to a search for other relevant adoption data that compared home environment and IQ in adoptive and nonadoptive families (Plomin et al., 1985). Three adoption studies were found and their data, examined for the first time from this perspective, consistently support the hypothesis of genetic mediation (Burks, 1928; Freeman, Holzinger, & Mitchell, 1928; Leahy, 1935). Across the three studies, the average correlation between environmental measures and children's IQ is .45 in nonadoptive families and .18 in adoptive families. However, unlike the HOME, which attempts to assess proximal features of the home environment, the environmental measures employed in the earlier studies largely assessed socioeconomic status (SES). For this reason, these earlier studies might be better viewed as indicating that the genetic overlap between SES and children's IQ is largely due to passive GE correlation.

## MEASURES OF FAMILY ENVIRONMENT
## AS RELATED TO OTHER DEVELOPMENTAL MEASURES

The method to assess genetic mediation due to measured passive GE correlation was developed because, in the Colorado Adoption Project, correlations between environmental measures and behavioral measures, when they emerged, were consistently greater in nonadoptive than in adoptive families (Plomin & DeFries, 1985). If an environmental measure is not correlated with a behavioral measure, the correlation cannot show genetic mediation. In the first report on such analyses in infancy (Plomin et al., 1985), from hundreds of environment-development correlations, 34 were selected in which the correlation reached statistical significance in either adoptive or nonadoptive families. Of the 34 correlations, 28 yielded greater correlations in nonadoptive than in adoptive families. For all 34 correlations, the mean correlation for nonadoptive families was .24; for adoptive families, the mean correlation was .09. Furthermore, the correlations in adoptive and nonadoptive families were significantly different for 12 comparisons. For all 12, the correlations in the nonadoptive families were greater than those in adoptive families. This consistent pattern of greater correlations in nonadoptive than in adoptive families suggests genetic links between the environmental measures and major domains of infant development that are due to passive GE correlation. These genetic links are not limited to a particular environmental measure nor to a particular domain of development. In general, the HOME correlates genetically with cognitive and language measures, as discussed above, and the FES correlates with temperament and behavioral problems. For example, correlations between the FES Personal Growth factor and Difficult Temperament were greater in nonadoptive families than in adoptive families at both 1 year (−.32 vs. −.07) and 3 years (−.28 vs. −.11). Several other similar findings suggest that genetic effects on familial "warmth" (cohesiveness and expressiveness) in part involve the mechanism of passive GE correlation as mediated by infant "easiness" (low difficultness and emotionality and high sociability and soothability). Longitudinal correlations between the FES at 1 year and later behavioral measures are generally weaker but show similar patterns of results (Plomin, DeFries, & Fulker, 1988). An extension of this longitudinal approach predicted noncognitive outcomes in middle childhood from early environment (Neiderhiser, in press). However, the phenotypic associations were weak and for this reason few genetic mediators were found. As mentioned earlier, the FES in infancy shows genetic links to children's IQ in middle childhood (Coon et al., 1990).

As discussed in the previous section, a tentative finding of considerable interest is that genetic effects on the HOME in infancy overlap with genetic effects on tester ratings of task orientation on the Infant Behavior Record. Is this genetic mediation due to passive GE correlation? The answer appears to be no. The correlation between the HOME and Task Orientation is .28 in nonadoptive families and .27 in adoptive families, suggesting shared family environmental influence but not genetic effects

(Braungart, in press). Taken together, these results suggest that, unlike other analyses, genetic mediation found in this multivariate genetic analysis is not due to passive GE correlation. This implies that it is due to reactive or active GE correlation. This seems reasonable given the nature of the IBR Task Orientation scale, which assesses responsiveness to objects, attention span, and goal directedness. That is, parents' responsiveness might reflect genetically influenced differences among infants in such behaviors. However, until these results are replicated, caution is warranted in making too much of the finding.

Although characteristics of the children are related genetically to the HOME and FES in infancy, genetic links due to passive GE correlation have not been found between parents' ratings of their warmth toward their children at 7 and 9 years and earlier tester ratings of temperament (Braungart, in press).

In summary, environmental measures in infancy share some genetic variance with noncognitive as well as cognitive characteristics of children. Although some of this genetic overlap involves passive GE correlation, some appears to reflect reactive and active GE correlation.

PARENTAL MEDIATORS OF PASSIVE GE CORRELATION

Demonstrating the importance of passive GE correlation raises the question of parental mediators of genetic links between the HOME and the Bayley. That is, children do not inherit family environments—they inherit genetically influenced predispositions of their parents. Thus, it must be the case that the genetic contribution to environmental measures generated by passive GE correlation involves some genetically mediated characteristics of parents that are inherited by their offspring. G in Figure 4.5 includes any characteristics of parents—including unmeasured and even unmeasurable characteristics—involved in the genetic link between the HOME and Bayley.

What are these parental characteristics that mediate passive GE correlation? As an example, we can investigate the extent to which the genetic link between the HOME and Bayley is due to the most likely parental candidate, parental IQ. This question can be addressed in simple analyses that partial out parental characteristics from the relationships between environmental measures and child characteristics in nonadoptive and adoptive families. For example, partialling out parental IQ has little effect on the relationships between the HOME and Bayley in either nonadoptive or adoptive homes (Plomin et al., 1985). For example, the HOME-Bayley correlation of .42 in nonadoptive families was only reduced to .41 when mothers' IQ was controlled and similarly to .41 when fathers' IQ was controlled (Bergeman & Plomin, 1988). In other words, parental characteristics involved in the passive GE correlation between the HOME and Bayley must be largely independent of the parents' IQ. Indeed, partialling out parental SES, education, IQ, specific cognitive abilities, and major dimensions of personality had little effect on genetic mediation of the HOME-Bayley relationship (Bergeman & Plomin, 1988).

This finding carries a straightforward implication for environmental research. It has been reasonably assumed that parental IQ must be the parental mediator of the relationship between the HOME and infant mental development (e.g., Gottfried & Gottfried, 1984; Yeates, MacPhee, Campbell, & Ramey, 1983). However, these results indicate that parental IQ is not the missing link.

Similar results have been obtained for domains other than cognitive development. For example, partialling out parental personality does not weaken the evidence for passive GE correlation for children's temperament. This suggests that the obvious candidate of parental personality is not responsible for the genetic links between environmental measures and children's temperament that are forged by passive GE correlation. Of course, one could always argue that the wrong traits have been examined as candidates. Some other "factor X" might be the key parental mediator of passive GE correlation that leads to genetic effects on environmental measures. Two redoubtable restrictions exist for finding parental mediators. First, the measure must not correlate highly with the parental measures listed above, and, second, it must correlate highly with both the environmental measure and the outcome measure. A stimulating discussion of possible parental mediators can be found in a recent book on parenting even though the book does not mention heredity (Goodnow & Collins, 1990). Directions for research include cognitive approaches such as information processing (e.g., Mancuso & Lehrer, 1986) and attribution (e.g., Dix & Grusec, 1983, 1985) in addition to affective approaches (Goodnow & Collins, 1990).

Although some "factor X" may be found to be the key parental mediator of passive GE correlation, a more interesting possibility is that genetic effects on other psychological traits of parents cannot explain all genetic effects on environmental measures. That is, genetic effects on environmental measures may not just be a matter of contamination by genetically influenced traits. This may lead to new ways of thinking about the interface between genes and experience.

For example, in 1875 Galton foreshadowed passive GE correlation and proposed an interesting hypothesis about genetic mediation. In response to the assumption that parental correlates of children's development can be ascribed to environmental influence, Galton wrote:

> I acknowledge the fact, but doubt the deduction. The child is usually taught by its parents, and their teachings are of an exceptional character, for the following reason. There is commonly a strong resemblance, owing to inheritance, between the dispositions of the child and its parents. They are able to understand the ways of one another more intimately than is possible to persons not of the same blood, and the child instinctively assimilates the habits and ways of thought of its parents. Its disposition is "educated" by them, in the true sense of the word; that is to say; it is evoked earlier than it would otherwise have been. On these grounds, I ascribe the persistence of habits that date from the early periods of home education, to the peculiarities of the instructors, rather than to the period when the instruction was given. The marks left on the memory by the instructions of a foster-mother are soon sponged clean away. (Galton, 1875, p. 405)

This remarkably prescient statement indicates that environment-outcome associations can be genetically mediated via passive GE correlation. Galton even foreshadows the passive GE correlation design described in this section that rests on the comparison of environment-outcome associations in nonadoptive and adoptive families. However, the special relevance of this quote to the present discussion is Galton's suggestion that passive GE correlation comes about because the genetic resemblance between parents and offspring enables them to "understand the ways of one another more intimately than is possible to persons not of the same blood." Galton's concept of intimacy has not been investigated but serves as an intriguing example of new ways of thinking about family environment in relation to passive GE correlation. This is a topic to which we shall return in the next chapter.

BEYOND THE FAMILY ENVIRONMENT

It would be reasonable to assume that passive GE correlation will be seen only in relation to family environment. That is, correlations between extrafamilial environmental measures and behavioral measures would not be expected to be greater for nonadopted than for adopted children. However, it is possible that effects of passive GE correlation spread to experiences beyond the family. Some surprising results of this type have emerged in the Colorado Adoption Project (Rende, in press). A self-report measure of stress in the first grade was correlated with teacher reports of behavioral problems on the Child Behavior Checklist (CBCL) in first grade and 2 years later. As shown in Table 4.3, correlations between stress and behavioral problems were greater for nonadopted children than for adopted children. This result emerged for total number of stressful events and was even stronger for a rating of the total upsettingness of the events. Similar results were found for internalizing and externalizing behavioral problems. Moreover, the effect was stronger 2 years later.

Although this finding needs to be replicated, it serves as an example of the possible role of passive GE correlation in measures of the environment that extend beyond the family. If these results are replicable, passive GE correlation provides a reasonable explanation of these findings. Some genetically influenced characteristics of parents might mediate children's responses to the stress of school. A major complication, however, is that in this same report

**TABLE 4.3**  Passive GE Correlation: Correlations Between Child Report of First-Grade Stress and Teacher Reports of Behavior Problems in First Grade and 2 Years Later

|  | Nonadopted | | Adopted | |
|---|---|---|---|---|
|  | Total Events | Upset-tingness | Total Events | Upset-tingness |
| Internalizing Problems |  |  |  |  |
| First grade | .18 | .25 | .08 | .18 |
| Third grade | .21 | .33 | .03 | .05 |
| Externalizing Problems |  |  |  |  |
| First grade | .19 | .33 | .17 | .16 |
| Third grade | .22 | .40 | .09 | .06 |

SOURCE: Adapted from Rende (in press).
NOTE: $N = 206$ adopted and 208 nonadopted probands in first grade and 177 adopted and 169 nonadopted probands in third grade.

the measure of school stress shows no genetic contribution in a sibling adoption analysis. If the measure shows no genetic effects, it should not show passive GE correlation. Nonetheless, the differences in correlations for nonadoptive and adoptive families from the passive GE correlation design are sufficiently large to warrant further investigation.

## An Adoption Design to Detect Specific Reactive and Active GE Correlations

Multivariate genetic analysis of the association between environmental measures and behavioral measures assesses passive, reactive, and active GE correlation. The measured passive GE correlation design just discussed assesses passive GE correlation but not reactive or active GE correlation. Another adoption design is able to assess specific GE correlations of the reactive and active type but not passive GE correlation. Comparison of results from these three methods make it possible to begin to gauge the relative importance of the three types of GE correlation.

The adoption design to detect specific reactive and active GE correlation requires data from biological parents of adopted-away children. Characteristics of adoptees' biological parents can be used as an index of genotype and they can be correlated with any measure of their adopted-away children's environment inside or outside of the home (Plomin et al., 1977). If a measure such as IQ of the biological parent correlates with any measure of the environment of their adopted-away children, in the absence of selective placement, this suggests that IQ contributes genetically to the environmental measure for reasons of reactive or active GE correlation. For example, a correlation between biological parents' IQ and adopted children's experience indicates that the environment responds to the children's genotypes (reactive GE correlation) or that the children's genotype drives their experiences (active GE correlation). For this reason, this design could be called the *measured reactive/active GE correlation design*, in contrast to the measured passive GE correlation design described in the previous section.

Previous adoption studies do not permit the use of this approach because biological parents and adoptive home environments are rarely assessed. For example, the classic adoption study of Skodak and Skeels (1949) tested biological mothers for IQ but only obtained information on the educational levels and socioeconomic status of adoptive parents. These measures of the distal environment of adoptive families cannot be expected to change in reaction to (reactive GE correlation) or be changed by (active GE correlation) genetic propensities of adopted children.

The Colorado Adoption Project provides relevant comparisons because it includes environmental measures of the adoptive families such as the HOME and FES. However, attempts to find specific reactive and active GE correlation using this approach in infancy and early childhood have not yielded much solid evidence for reactive GE correlation (Plomin & DeFries, 1985; Plomin, DeFries, & Fulker, 1988). For example, biological mothers' IQ correlated −.02 with scores on the HOME in adoptive families when the adopted children were 1 year old. At 2 years, the correlation was .01. The data for early childhood also suggest little effect, although the correlations increase slightly: .05 at 3 years and .07 at 4 years.

One might expect that, of the specific cognitive abilities, an adoptee's propensity toward verbal ability might elicit greater responsiveness in the adoptive family. However, correlations between biological mothers' verbal ability and HOME scores were also low at 1, 2, 3, and 4 years (.01, .04, .06, and .00, respectively), as were GE correlations for other specific cognitive abilities.

Overall, only slightly more than a chance number of significant GE correlations emerged. Nonetheless, the novelty of these data warrant a brief mention of the results. Of 20 GE correlations between biological mothers' personality and HOME scores from years 1 to 4, two were significant, both involving data at year 4. Adoptive mothers obtained higher HOME scores when the biological mothers of their adopted children were more highly active and impulsive (correlations of .16 and .17, respectively). Although it is not surprising that more lively children elicit greater responsiveness, the correlations at years 1, 2, and 3 were negligible, −.04, −.03, and .09, respectively for activity, and −.05, −.03, and −.02 for impulsivity. Thus, if this is truly an example of reactive/active GE correlation, it does not emerge until the children are 4 years old.

An interesting GE correlation also emerged at 4 years for biological mothers' self-reported depression. Adoptive mothers displayed less responsiveness as indexed by the HOME when biological mothers of their adopted children reported more depression (correlation of −.19). Again, however, correlations at earlier years were negligible: .06, .04, and .01.

The FES yielded only a chance number of significant correlations with biological mothers' IQ. However, the FES would appear to be less sensitive to change in response to a child's characteristics than the HOME because the FES assesses the general atmosphere of the family environment. Only a chance number of significant correlations were observed between biological mothers' personality and the adoptive families' FES. Nonetheless, there were some noteworthy consistencies at 1 and 3 years, the two ages when the FES was administered. The second-order FES factor Traditional Organization correlated .13 with biological mothers' 16PF Extraversion at year 1 and .07 at year 3. This hints at the possibility that a genetic propensity toward extraversion (which includes impulsivity as well as sociability) in children elicits greater parental control. The second-order FES factor Personal Growth correlated –.12 and –.08 at 1 and 3 years, respectively, with biological mothers' 16PF Neuroticism. Perhaps a genetic tendency toward neuroticism in children leads parents to be less warm and expressive. Another consistent pattern of results emerged for a measure of fearfulness. Correlations between biological mothers' self-reported fearfulness and adoptive parents' ratings of FES Traditional Organization were –.15 at 1 year and –.12 at 3 years, suggesting that parents exercise less control when their children are prone to being fearful. Possibly related to this is the finding that biological mothers' self-reported depression correlated –.07 and –.11 at 1 and 3 years with FES Traditional Organization.

Stepping back from these hints of active and reactive GE correlation, the larger picture shows few significant GE correlations using this method, these measures, and the young ages in the Colorado Adoption Project. The approach will detect GE correlation only when there is a heritable relationship between the phenotype of the biological mother and that of the adopted child and when there is a relationship between the environmental measure in the adopted family and the adopted child's phenotype. Although these appear to be quite restrictive limitations, they actually define GE correlation: Genetic differences among children are correlated with differences in their environments. One real limitation in the Colorado Adoption Project is that the genotype of adopted children needs to be estimated from characteristics of biological parents. This is a weak index of the adopted child's genotype for two reasons. First, parents and offspring are first-degree relatives whose coefficient of genetic relatedness is only .50. Second, biological parents are adults and the adopted children are young, which means that changes in genetic effects from childhood to adulthood will also dilute this index of the children's genotype. Another limitation is that the environmental measures yield few strong relationships with children's phenotypes. GE correlation will not be detected unless there is a relationship between the environmental measure and the adopted child's phenotype in addition to a heritable relationship between the phenotype of the biological parents and their adopted-away children. Nonetheless, taking the data at face value, it appears that passive GE correlation is a stronger force than reactive and active GE correlation in terms of mediating the genetic contribution to environmental measures. This tentative conclusion is limited to data from the Colorado Adoption Project, which have been analyzed only in infancy and early childhood. As discussed in the next chapter, a developmental theory of genetics and experience predicts that the reactive and active forms of GE correlation become more important as children experience environments outside the family and begin to play a more active role in the selection and creation of their environments.

## Summary

How do measures of the environment come to show a genetic contribution? These first attempts to search for mediators of this genetic contribution have uncovered some interesting possibilities. Multivariate genetic analysis can assess the extent to which covariance between an environmental measure and a behavioral measure is mediated genetically. Moreover, multivariate genetic analysis detects genetic sources of covariance due to any kind of GE correlation—passive, reactive, or active.

A general hypothesis is beginning to emerge from multivariate genetic analyses of this type: Phenotypic covariance between an environmental measure and traditional trait measures is typically due in part, but only in part, to genetic mediation.

This hypothesis has three implications. First, we can speed up the search for mediators of the genetic contribution to environmental measures by screening behavioral measures for phenotypic correlations with the environmental measures. Although a multivariate genetic analysis is needed to pin down the extent to which phenotypic correlations between environmental measures and trait measures are mediated genetically, so far the phenotypic results follow a reasonable pattern. When an environmental measure and a behavioral measure are both moderately heritable, as is typically the case, the phenotypic correlation between them is mediated in part by genetic factors. Turning this around, it is likely that a phenotypic correlation between an environmental measure and a behavioral measure is mediated in part by genetic factors. An important corollary of this point is that predictions of outcomes from environmental measures are likely to be mediated in part genetically. A book could be written about this topic, especially given its obvious implications for applied issues. Most importantly, it cannot be assumed that correlations between environmental measures and measures of outcomes are mediated entirely by environmental factors. "Outcome" measures are not necessarily causal outcomes of the environmental measure. For example, correlations between measures of family environment and children's development could be due to genetic rather than environmental factors, especially when family members are related genetically. As mentioned earlier in this chapter, the strategic focus here has been on genetic correlates of environmental measures. The agnostic word *correlate* sidesteps the causal arguments about whether certain measures are antecedents or consequences of an environmental measure.

Second, to the extent that genetic effects on environmental measures can be explained by genetically influenced behavioral measures, this suggests that purer measures of the environment can be created. That is, environmental measures could be constructed to be independent of these characteristics of the individual and thus freed from genetic effects. This can be accomplished statistically by partialling out the trait, but it will be accomplished better by constructing environmental measures that do not show genetic overlap with these characteristics. Success in constructing purer measures of the environment will depend on knowing more about why certain traits are genetically related to certain facets of the environment. The third implication rests on the "but not all" phrase. In the research on genetic mediators described in this chapter, it appears that traditional trait measures may not be able to account for most genetic effects on environmental measures.

This unexplained genetic contribution may be the most interesting, an issue taken up in the next chapter. Research reviewed in this chapter suggests another, even more tentative, hypothesis. In addition to multivariate genetic analysis, which can detect genetic mediation due to passive, reactive, or active GE correlation, two other genetic analyses were described that are more limited in scope than multivariate genetic analysis. One of these methods can detect only passive GE correlation and the other is limited to reactive and active GE correlation. Thus by comparing the results for the three methods it is possible to sort out the type of GE correlation responsible for genetic mediation. This is relevant to understanding the mechanisms by which genetic mediation arises. That is, if passive GE correlation is important, we need to look toward genetically influenced characteristics of parents that are correlated both with the environment they provide their children and with genetic influences on their children's traits. To the extent that reactive and active GE correlation is involved, we need to consider genetically influenced characteristics of children to which other people react (reactive GE correlation) and that lead children toward niche-picking and niche-building (active GE correlation).

The conclusion that emerges from preliminary work in this vein is rather surprising. Although reactive and active GE correlation seem intuitively to be most important in terms of genetic effects on experience, the initial research described in this chapter suggests that passive GE correlation may be most important.

This conclusion has three implications as well. First, because passive GE correlation involves the effect of receiving correlated genes and environments from parents, it motivates a search for parental mediators, not just child mediators, of genetic effects on environmental measures. Here our path through this new territory disappears. Traditional trait measures of parents do not appear to be able to account for this genetic link. Again, this may lead to new ways of thinking about the interface between genes and experience. Francis Galton may have been on the right trail more than a century ago in suggesting that genetically induced intimacy between parent and child might be involved.

The second implication comes from noting that the evidence for passive GE correlation rests entirely on research with infants and young children. The implication is that we need to consider a prediction from the GE correlation theory of development proposed by Scarr and McCartney (1983). They predict that the impact of passive GE correlation wanes and reactive and active GE correlation increases in importance during development as children become increasingly able to modify, select, and create their environments. This developmental theory of GE correlation is elaborated in the next chapter.

The third implication comes from the realization that our measures of the environment are typically passive measures. If we are to find reactive and active GE correlations, which seem to lie at the heart of the genetic interface with experience, we need measures of the environment that move beyond the outdated view of the child as a passive receptacle for environmental deposits to a reactive view and, especially, to an active view of the child's role in experience. These issues are the topic of the next, and last, chapter.

# 5

# Nature-Nurture and Experience

This book began with a dispute between geneticists 40 years ago. Darlington assumed that genetic factors affect individuals' selection and creation of environments. Dobzhansky and Penrose charged casuistry because Darlington had no data to back up his assertion. Chapters 2 and 3 provided the data that Darlington needed: Genetic factors contribute to many widely used measures of familial and extrafamilial environments.

What mediates the genetic contribution to environmental measures? Three hypotheses can be drawn from research reviewed in the previous chapter. First, specific mediators can be found using multivariate genetic analyses. Second, GE correlation responsible for this genetic mediation appears to be due primarily to the passive type of GE correlation rather than the reactive and active types, at least during early childhood. Third, most of the genetic contribution to environmental measures is not explained by traditional trait measures.

This final chapter begins with a discussion of the second and third issues. Why does GE correlation appear to be passive rather than reactive and active? What accounts for the rest of the genetic contribution to environmental measures? The last part of the chapter formalizes an emerging theory of genetics and experience.

## GE Correlation and Development

It would be surprising if passive GE correlation rather than the reactive and active types of GE correlation governed the interface between nature and nurture. Passive GE correlation is interesting conceptually, especially for family researchers. For example, Galton's hypothesis of genetically induced intimacy is intriguing. However, the passivity of passive GE correlation is bothersome, as is the fact that it is limited to interactions among genetically related individuals. Reactive and active types of GE correlation are more compatible with contemporary views of transactions between organism and environment. Moreover, these types of GE correlation are not limited to family members.

Although it may be the case that, like it or not, GE correlation is primarily of the passive type, it seems reasonable to propose that reactive and especially active GE correlation become more important as children experience environments outside the family and play a more active role in the selection and creation of their environments. The evidence that the genetic contribution to environmental measures is due to passive rather than active and reactive GE correlation rests on adoption analyses of young children. This leaves open the possibility that active and reactive GE correlation becomes increasingly important later in development.

This is the developmental theory proposed by Sandra Scarr and Kathleen McCartney in 1983 prior to the past decade's accumulating evidence for genetic effects on environmental measures:

> The relative importance of the three kinds of genotype → environment effects changes with development. The influence of the passive kind declines from infancy to adolescence, and the importance of the active kind increases over the same period. (Scarr & McCartney, 1983, p. 427)

The expression "genotype → environment" was used by Scarr and McCartney to signify the developmental processes of GE correlation rather than the quantitative genetic component of variance called GE correlation. However, the arrow between genotype and environment conveys a causality that goes beyond the correlation between genotypes and environment. Although at one point in their article Scarr and McCartney indicated that their theory "implies a probabilistic connection between a person and the environment" (p. 428), their theme was that "genes drive experience" (p. 425). The evidence reviewed in this book suggests that genes contribute to environmental measures, but most of the variance of these measures is not genetic in origin. In other words, the evidence suggests that genes contribute to but do not determine experience.

One does not have to agree with the causal interpretation of genotype → environment in order to appreciate the interesting developmental features of this theory of GE correlation. Most importantly, the theory makes a straightforward prediction: Greater evidence for active GE correlation should be found in adolescence. The prediction will be testable, for example, as children in the Colorado Adoption Project, now in middle childhood (DeFries et al., in press), reach adolescence.

It is possible that passive GE correlation will loom large, even in adolescence, as long as we continue to assess the environment using a passive model in which the child is a mere receptacle for the environment—for example, assessing what parents do to their children. The emphasis on the active experience of the child is a component of developmentalists' long-standing interest in the child's role in the back-and-forth of developmental transactions between the organism and environment (Bell, 1968, 1979; Sameroff & Chandler, 1975). However, perhaps because this is such a reasonable notion, it jumped to the status of received wisdom without much research aimed at actually assessing it. As Harry McGurk recently noted:

> It is one thing, however, to acknowledge the mutuality of parental effects upon children and children's effects upon parents. It is quite

another to address the complex conceptual, theoretical, methodological and measurement issues that arise whenever the analysis of such effects is contemplated. (McGurk, 1992, p. 243)

McGurk's comment was in response to a paper (Russell & Russell, 1992) that resurrects the issue of bidirectionality of effects in parent-child interactions and attempts to explore the processes that underlie child effects (albeit without discussing genetics). Research along these lines will contribute to exploration of the interface between nature and nurture. The rate-limiting step is the dearth of measures of the environment that go beyond the passive model.

## Experience

Research reviewed in the previous chapter identified some traits that partially mediate the genetic contribution to environmental measures. However, most of the genetic contribution remains unexplained by standard psychological traits. Of course, it can always be argued that the wrong traits have been examined as candidates, that some "factor X" is the key mediator of genetic effects on environmental measures. For example, optimism, the personality moniker for seeing the world through rose-colored glasses, is a dimension that has only recently been considered in genetic research. Optimism is heritable (Plomin et al., 1992) and predicts mental and physical health variables (Seligman, 1991; Taylor, 1989). For these reasons, optimism is a reasonable candidate for mediation of genetic effects on environmental measures, especially for those measures that rely on perceptions of the environment. Readers are likely to have their own favorite factor X candidates.

Although some factor X may be found to be the key mediator of the genetic contribution for a particular measure of the environment, a more profound possibility is that genetic effects on other psychological traits cannot explain all genetic effects on environmental measures. That is, the genetic contribution to environmental

measures might not just be a matter of contamination by genetically influenced traits. Rather, experience itself may be influenced
by genetic factors.

One concrete example is peers. As discussed in Chapter 3,
measures of peer characteristics in adolescence appear to show
greater heritability than measures of family environment. Unlike
parents, peers are seldom imposed on children. Children select
their peers and are selected by them. Children also modify the
characteristics of their peer groups. Could it be that the greater
heritability of characteristics of peer groups is due to the reactive
and active nature of this extrafamilial environmental factor that is
so salient to adolescent life?

The search for active models of the environment ought not to be
limited to such macro-environmental social addresses as peer groups
or middle-class pigeonholes such as ballet lessons. Darlington's
book was attacked by Dobzhansky and Penrose as too determinis-
tic. Specifically, they attacked the idea that genetic factors affect the
environments we choose: "Does the author really believe that man
is free to choose or to create his environment?" (Dobzhansky &
Penrose, 1955, p. 77). Dobzhansky and Penrose meant that we are
not free to choose the womb in which we are born or the school
that we attend. Children have little choice about their embryolog-
ical address or their social address, but the environment consists
of more than such macro-environmental social addresses. Children are able to choose or create the micro-environments that form
the bulk of their immediate experience. For example, what do
children see when they look at the corner of a room? Nothing?
White paint? Or an interesting geometric conversion of lines and
angles?

Socially as well as cognitively, children select, modify, and even
create their experiences. Children select environments that are
rewarding or at least comfortable, *niche-picking*. Children modify
their environments by setting the background tone for interactions, by initiating behavior, and by altering the impact of environments (Buss & Plomin, 1984). Children can make their own
environments. That is, they can create environments compatible

with their propensities, *niche-building*. Bright children can use the stimulus of an empty room to think about the geometric configuration of its corners.

Research on the active selection, modification, and creation of environments might be fostered by using a word other than *environment*. At least historically, *environment* connotes events that impinge on a passive organism, like the stimulus in stimulus-response theory. The word *experience* might be helpful conceptually because of its connotation of active involvement of the organism (McGue et al., 1991). Dictionaries define *experience* very differently, but most emphasize two components: apprehension of an event and direct participation in an event.

Experience as apprehension of an event connotes cognitive construction, which, as discussed in Chapter 1, is a central feature of O-S-R models of environment. Cognitive constructionist views have emerged in most areas of psychology. For example, the behavioral geneticist Sandra Scarr (1992) has argued for a constructivist view in which children's "constructed realities" importantly determine their experiences: "In this view, human experience is the construction of reality, not a property of a physical world that imparts the same experience to everyone who encounters it" (Scarr, 1992, p. 5). Decades ago, the personality theorist Henry Murray emphasized that people construct personal myths to give coherence to their lives (Kluckholm, Murray, & Schneider, 1953). Social psychology has shifted dramatically toward cognitive construction (Ross & Nisbett, 1991). The new field of cultural psychology is based on the proposition that sociocultural environments depend on the meaning people give to them (Shweder, 1990).

Self-report or interview measures of the environment such as life events or the family environment are, in a way, measures of "apprehension of events." Are more objective measures of "direct participation in events" possible? It is much more difficult to study children's active use of environments than it is to assess the environment to which a child is passively exposed. It is not clear to me what objective measures of active experience would even look like, although some of their formal features are obvious: To study selection, choices must be investigated; to study modification, the target is changes in environments wrought by children; to study creation of environments, the focus is children's use of the environment. The issues are deeper than those involving appropriate assessment of the environment in order to assess children's active use of the environment. For example, the hoary issue of motivation might need to be resurrected. The personality theorist Gordon Allport (1937) asked, "What is it that sets the stream of activity into motion, that sustains it until it lapses or changes?" His answer is that "this is the problem of motivation, and there is no problem in psychology more difficult to handle" (p. 110). Allport's concept of functional autonomy may be useful: "A person likes to do what he can do well" (p. 201). Other cognitive-motivational constructs may also be useful, such as effectance motivation (White, 1959) and intrinsic motivation (Hunt, 1965). There are signs of a return to motivation, for example, in the role of interest in cognitive development (Renninger, Hidi, & Krapp, 1992).

Bouchard and his colleagues (Bouchard et al., 1990; Bouchard, Lykken, Tellegen, & McGue, in press) are developing a motivational theory called Experience-Producing Drives-Revised (EPD-R). They credit the core construct to Hayes (1962). Using intelligence as an example, Hayes proposed that genetic influence "consists of tendencies to engage in activities conducive to learning, rather than inherited intellectual capacities, as such. These tendencies are referred to here as experience-producing drives (EPD's)" (Hayes, 1962, p. 337). Hayes's theory postulated multiple drives and a single general learning capacity. The EPD revision of Bouchard et al. proposes instead "that what drives behavior and subsequent experience are mechanisms that involve specialized structural features of the brain, mechanisms that account for both capacity and drive" (Bouchard et al., in press).

So far, EPD-R theory has focused on universal features of development: "The theoretical point is that the necessary environments for bringing most human traits and skills to a functional level are, as Scarr has argued, widely present and can be readily acquired by a motivated child" (Bouchard et al., in press). Although they suggest that ubiquitous genetic variation could be caused by constraints on selection of these mechanisms, bridging the gap between species-typical and species-variable genetic influences is difficult, as discussed in Chapter 1 in relation to the selection versus instruction debate. Also, a critic might carp that the use of the word *drive* merely gives a name to what we do not know and seems to connote something suspiciously similar to the even hoarier word *instinct*. Still, I find the theory's emphasis on motivation thought provoking. Also, like other positions mentioned in this section, the theory emphasizes that "human beings create their own environments and thus control, to some extent, their own experiences" (Bouchard et al., in press).

## A Theory of Genetics and Experience

To a child with a new hammer, everything looks like a nail. I admit to looking at the world of the nature-nurture hyphen from one particular perspective. My excuse is that it has been useful in the history of science for a proponent to take a new concept as far as it will go, knowing that, especially in the arena of behavioral genetics, there is never a dearth of critics whose own hammers are at the ready to ensure that one does not go too far. The goal of this section is to be explicit about the theory of genetics and experience that has emerged in this book.

The word *theory* is used here to connote a system to describe, predict, and explain these nature-nurture phenomena. At the least, a theory should describe, organize, and condense existing facts in a reasonable, internally consistent manner. A theory should also make predictions concerning phenomena not yet investigated and allow clear tests of these predictions. At their best, theories explain phenomena as well as describe and predict them.

The following seven hypotheses represent an empirically based theory of genetics and experience meant to be testable and falsifiable.

1. GENETIC DIFFERENCES AMONG INDIVIDUALS
CONTRIBUTE TO MEASURES OF THE ENVIRONMENT

The empirical foundation for this book is the research reviewed in Chapters 2 and 3, which make the case that widely used measures of the environment show significant and substantial genetic effects. Genetic effects emerge from adoption as well as twin studies, from child-based as well as parent-based genetic designs, from research employing observations as well as self-reports, and from research on extrafamilial environments as well as familial environments.

This hypothesis does not imply that all measures of the environment show genetic effects or that all of the variance of environmental measures is genetic in origin. For example, the research reviewed in Chapter 2 suggests that measures of parental control in child-based genetic designs show lower heritability than other measures of parenting. Moreover, the research reviewed in Chapters 2 and 3 clearly shows that most of the variance in environmental measures is not genetic in origin. However, it is not news that environmental measures show some environmental influence. The news is that widely used environmental measures show significant genetic effects. Another issue should be emphasized: Research on the genetics of experience, as in any genetic research on complex dimensions and disorders, does not imply genetic determinism. It refers to probabilistic propensities rather than predetermined programming.

The main implication of this finding for developmentalists is that environmental measures cannot be assumed to be environmental just because they are called environmental. To the contrary, research to date suggests that it is safer to assume that ostensible measures of the environment include genetic effects. Research on environmental influences, especially research in families consisting of genetically related individuals, will profit from using genetically sensitive designs in order to disentangle environmental and genetic threads in the fabric of family life.

## 2. THE GENETIC CONTRIBUTION TO MEASURES OF THE ENVIRONMENT IS GREATER FOR MEASURES OF ACTIVE EXPERIENCE

As discussed in Chapter 1, environmental theory has moved away from passive ("stimulus") models to active ("organism-stimulus-response," O-S-R) models that recognize the active role of children in selecting, modifying, and creating their own environments. Nonetheless, extant environmental measures are much more passive than active. Although many of these measures of the environment as stimulus show genetic influence, it seems reasonable to predict that O-S-R measures will show greater genetic influence. As mentioned earlier in this chapter, the strong genetic influence on characteristics of children's peer groups might reflect children's ability to select their peers, in contrast to their ability to select their parents or siblings. A more obvious example comes from research on life events reviewed in Chapter 3. Items on measures of life events for which the individual has greater control show greater genetic influence. The evidence for this hypothesis is admittedly weak, but the reason for this is that measures of the environment are still largely passive in their orientation despite the clear advance of environmental theory toward more active models.

## 3. THE GENETIC CONTRIBUTION TO MEASURES OF THE ENVIRONMENT IS DUE IN PART TO PSYCHOLOGICAL TRAITS

Multivariate genetic research indicates that some genetic effects on measures of the environment can be explained by genetic effects on psychological traits such as personality, psychopathology, and cognitive abilities. Just as finding some genetic contribution to environmental measures does not imply that genetic factors explain all of the variance of these measures, finding some genetic contribution to the covariance between environmental measures and behavioral traits does not imply that all of the covariance is genetic in origin. It should be reiterated that environmental measures, even those with a significant genetic contribution, can of course be associated with behavioral measures environmentally, not genetically. Documenting environmental contributions to this covariance is critically important for environmental research on prediction, prevention, and intervention. The book focuses on the genetic contribution to this covariance because of the light it sheds on behavioral characteristics that might mediate the genetic role in environmental measures.

The main implication of this finding for behavioral geneticists is that genetic research on behavioral traits can gain a new dimension by including measures of the environment. Multivariate genetic analyses can then be conducted that investigate the extent to which behavioral traits mediate the genetic contribution to environmental measures. For developmentalists, the main implication is that purer measures of the environment could be created by constructing environmental measures independent of these genetically influenced characteristics.

The phrase *in part* in this hypothesis is the crux of the next hypothesis.

4. GENETIC DIFFERENCES AMONG INDIVIDUALS
CONTRIBUTE TO DIFFERENCES IN EXPERIENCE
INDEPENDENT OF PSYCHOLOGICAL TRAITS

Multivariate genetic analyses suggest that some genetic effects on measures of the environment cannot be explained by genetic effects on psychological traits. The evidence for this hypothesis is weak because the hypothesis asserts the null hypothesis. That is, it is always possible to argue that some as yet unstudied factor X might eventually explain the genetic contribution to measures of the environment. Nonetheless, the evidence as it stands supports the hypothesis. The hypothesis warrants attention because of its interesting implications. Genetic effects on environmental measures may be more than a matter of mediation by genetically influenced psychological traits: Experience itself, how we interact with our environments, may be influenced by genetic factors.

## 5. GENETIC FACTORS CONTRIBUTE TO LINKS BETWEEN ENVIRONMENTAL MEASURES AND DEVELOPMENTAL OUTCOMES

Given that environmental measures as well as outcome measures show genetic effects, it seems reasonable that links between environmental measures and developmental outcomes may be mediated genetically. Of course, even if genetic factors contribute substantially to an environmental measure, the measure could nonetheless relate to an outcome solely for environmental reasons. Multivariate genetic analyses of the covariance between environmental measures and outcome measures are needed to disentangle genetic and environmental contributions to the covariance. Multivariate genetic research reviewed in the preceding chapter provides examples of such genetic mediation. For example, genetic factors have been implicated in the relationship between home environment and children's later development and between life events and later depression. This research was discussed in terms of genetic correlates of environmental measures, using the agnostic word *correlate* to sidestep causal arguments about whether "outcome" measures are truly causal consequences of an environmental measure.

## 6. PROCESSES UNDERLYING GENETIC CONTRIBUTIONS TO EXPERIENCE CHANGE DURING DEVELOPMENT

Passive genotype-environment (GE) correlation appears to be surprisingly powerful in infancy and childhood, at least for the sorts of family environmental measures currently available. Scarr's theory suggests that, by adolescence, passive GE correlation diminishes and active GE correlation increases in importance as children select their own experiences. Progress in understanding this shift from passive to active GE correlation—indeed, progress for the entire field of genetics and experience—depends on developing measures of children's active selection, modification, and creation of experience.

## 7. SPECIFIC GENES THAT AFFECT EXPERIENCE WILL BE IDENTIFIED

This last hypothesis has not been mentioned previously in this book because there is as yet no evidence to support it. The breathtaking advances in molecular genetics during the past two decades have made it possible to begin to identify some of the many genes likely to be responsible for genetic variance in complex traits (Plomin, 1990b, 1993). Genetic research on experience will be revolutionized as we begin to replace anonymous components of variance assessed indirectly from twin and adoption studies with specific DNA assessed directly in individuals. In addition to identifying genes responsible for genetic variance in complex behavioral traits, the same approach can be applied to finding genes responsible for genetic variance in environmental measures. The long-term goal is to identify a set of DNA markers of genes that accounts for a substantial portion of the genetic variance for a particular measure of the environment.

This revolution will rewrite the six preceding hypotheses in terms of specific genes:

1. Specific genes will be identified that are associated with measures of the environment.
2. These genes are most likely to be found in association with measures of active experience rather than passive environments.
3. These genes will in part be associated with psychological traits.
4. These genes will in part be independent of psychological traits.
5. Genes associated with environmental measures will also be associated with outcome measures.
6. Genes will be identified that are associated with passive aspects of the environment in childhood, but later in development genes will be increasingly associated with active experience.

Identifying specific genes associated with measures of the environment will provide indisputable evidence of genetic effects on measures of the environment. It will also simplify several issues raised in this book. Three examples follow. First is the question raised in Chapter 2 whether finding greater MZ than DZ correlations for environmental measures should be interpreted as evidence of genetic effects or as a violation of the equal environments assumption of the twin method. The decision was that such results represent GE correlation and are therefore not a violation of the equal environments assumption. If a specific gene were found to be associated with an environmental measure in a sample of unrelated children, clearly this would be a genetic effect, not a violation of the equal environments assumption of the twin method.

A second example of the clarity that will come from the identification of specific genes concerns the comparison of child-based and parent-based genetic designs in analyses of the family environment as discussed in Chapter 2. It is difficult to think about the very different facets of the family environment that are engaged when, for example, parents' perceptions of the family environment are elicited in designs where twins are children (child-based genetic design) as compared to designs where the twins are the parents (parent-based genetic design). Consider a measure of parental perceptions of their affection toward their children. What would it mean if a specific gene were found to be associated with this measure using a child-based genetic design as compared to a parent-based genetic design? If such a gene-environment association were identified, the issue simply comes down to the question, whose gene is it? In the child-based design, it is the child's gene. The association of this gene in the child with parental perceptions of affection must be explained by gene-influenced characteristics of the child. For example, genetic effects on attributional processes of the parent cannot be involved except for a circuitous path involving passive GE correlation. In contrast, in a parent-based design, the gene identified is the parent's. This gene could be related to any genetically influenced characteristic of the parent including attributional processes involved in their perception.

A third example involves the research strategies used to detect the three types of GE correlation—passive, reactive, and active— as discussed in Chapter 4. If a specific gene were found to be associated with an environmental measure, which type of GE correlation would be responsible? Finding associations with specific genes is analogous to multivariate genetic analyses, in that such association can detect GE correlation of any type. However, gene-environment association can disentangle passive GE correlation from reactive and active GE correlation using the measured passive GE correlation design. In this case, the word *measured* refers both to the G and the E of GE correlation. If a gene-environment association were found for a measure of the family environment in nonadoptive families, this gene-environment association could represent passive as well as reactive or active GE correlation. However, if the association also emerged in adoptive families, it could not be due to passive GE correlation because adopted children do not inherit genes passively correlated with environments from their adoptive parents. Such an association in adoptive families must be attributed to reactive and active GE correlation. Adoptive parents might respond to characteristics of their adopted children associated with this gene (reactive GE correlation). Gene-associated characteristics of the adopted children may also underlie their attempts to use their parents to get what they want (active GE correlation).

This theory of genetics and experience meets the criteria of a theory described earlier. In addition, falsifiability is crucial and the theory meets this criterion as well. Each of the seven hypotheses can be proven wrong. The first hypothesis that posits a genetic contribution to environmental measures is unlikely to be completely wrong because of the consistent evidence that has accumulated in its favor. Still, these are early days in this new field. The generality of the hypothesis may prove to be more limited than current evidence suggests if future studies do not continue to find evidence for genetic contributions to other measures of the environment.

Some research can be construed as compatible with the second hypothesis—that active measures of experience will show greater genetic influence than passive measures of the environment. However, extant environmental measures are largely of the passive variety. Until ways to assess children's active role in selecting, modifying, and creating their environments are developed, this hypothesis will be difficult to test. Still, development of such measures of active experience should be the highest item on the environmental research agenda, not only to test this hypothesis, but to bring the empirical base of environmental research in line with modern environmental theory, as discussed in Chapter 1.

The third hypothesis—that some of the genetic contribution to environmental measures can be attributed to psychological traits— seems unlikely to be proven wrong because it is so reasonable and the first few studies along these lines provide strong support for it. Nonetheless, the hypothesis can be proven wrong if future multivariate genetic research is unable to identify psychological traits whose genetic variance overlaps with genetic variance for environmental measures.

The fourth hypothesis is and will remain weaker because it attempts to assert the null hypothesis that some genetic effects on environmental measures are independent of that for psychological traits. Nonetheless, the hypothesis is warranted by the far-reaching implication it conveys: Some genetic effects are unique to experience itself. It is a legitimate counterargument that some other previously unexamined trait might be found that explains genetic effects on a particular environmental measure. However, this hypothesis is consistent with the bits of research currently available. In the end, the burden of proof rests with the factor X proponents. They can prove this hypothesis wrong by multivariate genetic research that shows that all of the genetic variance on an environmental measure covaries with a trait measure or a set of trait measures.

The fifth hypothesis, that genetic factors in part mediate associations between environmental measures and outcome measures, has received some research support. It also follows from the finding that environmental measures as well as outcome measures show genetic effects. If both environmental and outcome measures are influenced genetically, associations between environmental measures and outcome measures can be mediated in part by genetic factors. However, because environmental measures and outcome measures are only partially influenced genetically, their association could be due to nongenetic influences. This hypothesis can be proven wrong by multivariate genetic research that shows that phenotypic associations between environmental measures and outcome measures are not mediated genetically.

The sixth hypothesis—that passive GE correlation gives way to active GE correlation during development—receives indirect support from the strong showing of passive GE correlation in childhood. However, despite the reasonableness of Scarr's hypothesis, it has not yet been shown that active GE correlation becomes increasingly important after adolescence. Although adoption designs are needed to disentangle passive, reactive, and active GE correlation, this hypothesis can be tested, for example, as children in the longitudinal Colorado Adoption Project reach adolescence. Moreover, the hypothesis can be explored preliminarily in nongenetic designs by assessing passive, reactive, and active aspects of experience and investigating their relationship with child characteristics during development.

There is as yet no evidence in support of the seventh hypothesis that specific genes associated with experience can be identified. The burden of proof clearly rests with people like me who believe that molecular genetics will revolutionize quantitative genetic research on complex phenomena, of which the interface between genetics and experience may be the most complex.

Even if some of these hypotheses are shown to be wrong, there can be little doubt that further exploration of the nature-nurture hyphen will provide interesting insights into the developmental processes by which genotypes become phenotypes.

# References

Allport, G. W. (1949). *Personality: A psychological interpretation.* London: Constable. (Original work published 1937)

Anastasi, A. (1958). Heredity, environment, and the question "How?" *Psychological Review, 65,* 197-208.

Baker, L. A., & Daniels, D. (1990). Nonshared environmental influences and personality differences in adult twins. *Journal of Personality and Social Psychology, 58,* 103-110.

Baron, R. M., & Kenny, D. A. (1986). The moderator-mediator variable distinction in social psychological research: Conceptual, strategic, and statistical considerations. *Journal of Personality and Social Psychology, 51,* 1173-1182.

Baumrind, D. (1993). The average expectable environment is not good enough: A response to Scarr. *Child Development, 64,* 1299-1317.

Beadle, G. W., & Tatum, E. L. (1941). Experimental control of developmental reaction. *American Naturalist, 75,* 107-116.

Bell, R. Q. (1968). A reinterpretation of the direction of effects in socialization. *Psychological Review, 75,* 81-95.

Bell, R. Q. (1979). Parent, child and reciprocal influences. *American Psychologist, 34,* 821-826.

Belsky, J. (1984). The determinants of parenting: A process model. *Child Development, 55,* 83-96.

Belsky, J. (1990). Parental and nonparental child care and children's socioemotional development. *Journal of Marriage and the Family, 52,* 885-903.

Bergeman, C. S., & Plomin, R. (1988). Parental mediators of the genetic relationship between home environment and infant mental development. *British Journal of Developmental Psychology, 6,* 11-19.

Bergeman, C. S., Plomin, R., Pedersen, N. L., & McClearn, G. E. (1991). Genetic mediation of the relationship between social support and psychological well-being. *Psychology and Aging, 6,* 640-646.

Bergeman, C. S., Plomin, R., Pedersen, N. L., McClearn, G. E., & Nesselroade, J. R. (1990). Genetic and environmental influences on social support: The Swedish Adoption/Twin Study of Aging (SATSA). *Journal of Gerontology, 45,* 101-106.

Berkman, L. F. (1983). The assessment of social networks and social support in the elderly. *Journal of the American Geriatrics Society, 31,* 743-749.

Black, I. B., Adler, J. E., Dreyfus, C. F., Friedman, W. F., LaGamma, E. F., & Roch, A. H. (1987). Biochemistry of information storage in the nervous system. *Science, 236,* 1263-1268.

Boomsma, D. I., & Molenaar, P. C. M. (1986). Using LISREL to analyze genetic and environmental covariance structure. *Behavior Genetics, 16,* 237-250.

Bornstein, M. (1989). Sensitive periods in development. *Psychological Bulletin, 105,* 179-197.

Bouchard, T. J., Jr. (in press). Genetic and environmental influences on adult personality: Evaluating the evidence. In J. Hettema & I. Deary (Eds.), *Basic issues in personality: European-American Workshop on Biological and Social Approaches to Individuality.* Dordecht: Kluwer.

Bouchard, T. J., Jr., Lykken, D. T., McGue, M., Segal, N. L., & Tellegen, A. (1990). Sources of human psychological difference: The Minnesota study of twins reared apart. *Science, 250,* 223-228.

Bouchard, T. J., Jr., Lykken, D. T., Tellegen, A., & McGue, M. (in press). Genes, drives, environment and experience: EPD theory—revised. In C. P. Benbow & D. Lubinski (Eds.), *From psychometrics to giftedness: Essays in honor of Julian C. Stanley.* Baltimore, MD: Johns Hopkins University Press.

Bouchard, T. J., Jr., & McGue, M. (1990). Genetic and rearing environmental influences on adult personality: An analysis of adopted twins reared apart. *Journal of Personality, 58,* 263-292.

Bradley, R., Caldwell, B., & Rock, S. (1988). Home environment and school performance: A ten year follow-up and examination of three models of environmental action. *Child Development, 59,* 852-867.

Bradley, R., Caldwell, B., Rock, S., Ramey, C., Barnard, K., Gray, C., Hammond, M., Mitchell, S., Gottfried, A., Siegel, L., & Johnson, D. (1989). Home environment and cognitive development in the first three years of life: A collaborative study involving six sites and three ethnic groups in North America. *Developmental Psychology, 25,* 217-235.

Bradley, R., Rock, S., Whiteside, L., Caldwell, B., Ramey, C., Barnard, K., Gray, C., Hammond, M., Mitchell, S., Gottfried, A., Siegel, L., & Johnson, D. (1990, April). *Early home environment and mental test performance: A structural analysis.* Paper presented to the International Society on Infant Studies, Montreal.

Braungart, J. M. (in press). Genetic influence on "environmental" measures. In J. C. DeFries, R. Plomin, & D. W. Fulker (Eds.), *Nature and nurture during middle childhood.* Cambridge, MA: Blackwell.

Braungart, J. M., Fulker, D. W., Plomin, R., & DeFries, J. C. (1992). Genetic influence of the home environment during infancy: A sibling adoption study of the HOME. *Developmental Psychology, 28,* 1048-1055.

Brett, J. F., Brief, A. P., Burke, M. J., George, J. M., & Webster, J. (1990). Negative affectivity and the reporting of stressful life events. *Health Psychology, 9,* 57-68.

Bronfenbrenner, U. (1977). Toward an experimental ecology of human development. *American Psychologist, 32,* 513-531.

Bronfenbrenner, U. (1989). Ecological systems theory. *Annals of Child Development, 6,* 187-249.

Bronfenbrenner, U. (in press). The ecology of cognitive development. In R. Wozniak & K. Fisher (Eds.), *Specific environments: Thinking in context.* Hillsdale, NJ: Lawrence Erlbaum.

Bronfenbrenner, U., & Ceci, S. J. (1983). Heredity, environment, and the question "how?" A first approximation. In R. Plomin & G. E. McClearn (Eds.), *Nature, nurture, and psychology* (pp. 313-324). Washington, DC: APA Books.

Bronfenbrenner, U., & Crouter, A. (1983). The evolution of environmental models in developmental research. In W. Kessen (Ed.), *Handbook of child psychology, Vol. 1,* (4th ed.) (pp. 357-414). New York: John Wiley.

Brown, G. W., & Harris, T. (1978). *The social origins of depression.* London: Tavistock.

Bryant, J. (Ed.). (1990). *Television and the American family.* Hillsdale, NJ: Lawrence Erlbaum.

Burks, B. (1928). The relative influence of nature and nurture upon mental development: A comparative study of foster parent-foster child resemblance and true parent-true child resemblance. *Twenty-Seventh Yearbook of the National Society for the Study of Education, 27,* 219-316.

Burnet, F. M. (1959). *The clonal selection theory of acquired immunity.* Cambridge: Cambridge University Press.

Buss, A. H., & Plomin, R. (1984). *Temperament: Early developing personality traits.* Hillsdale, NJ: Lawrence Erlbaum.

Buss, D. M., (1991). Evolutionary personality psychology. *Annual Review of Psychology, 42,* 459-491.

Caldwell, B. M., & Bradley, R. H. (1978). *Home Observation for Measurement of the Environment.* Little Rock: University of Arkansas.

Cardon, L., & Fulker, D. W. (1993). Genetics of specific cognitive abilities. In R. Plomin & G. E. McClearn (Eds.), *Nature, nurture, and psychology* (pp. 99-120). Washington, DC: APA Books.

Cattell, R. B. (1973). *Personality and mood by questionnaire.* San Francisco: Jossey-Bass.

Cattell, R. B. (1982). *The inheritance of personality and ability.* New York: Academic Press.

Caudill, W., & Weinstein, H. (1969). Maternal care and infant behavior in Japan and America. *Psychiatry, 32,* 12-43.

Cherny, S. S. (in press). Home environmental influences on general cognitive ability. In J. C. DeFries, R. Plomin, & D. W. Fulker (Eds.), *Nature and nurture during middle childhood.* Cambridge, MA: Blackwell.

Chipuer, H. M., Merriwether-Devries, C., & Plomin, R. (1993). *A genetic analysis of perceptions of the family environment: Nonadopted and adopted 7-year-olds and their parents.* Manuscript submitted for publication.

Chipuer, H. M., Plomin, R., Pedersen, N. L., McClearn, G. E., & Nesselroade, J. R. (1992). Genetic influence on family environment: The role of personality. *Developmental Psychology, 29,* 110-118.

Clarke, A., & Clarke, A. (1989). The later cognitive effects of early intervention. *Intelligence, 12,* 289-297.

Cohen, L. H., Towbes, L. C., & Flocco, R. (1988). Effects of induced mood on self-reported life events and perceived and received social support. *Journal of Personality and Social Psychology, 55,* 669-674.

Cohen, S., & Wills, T. A. (1985). Social support, stress and the buffering hypothesis. *Psychological Bulletin, 98*, 310-357.

Colombo, J. (1982). The critical period concept. *Psychological Bulletin, 91*, 260-275.

Coon, H., Fulker, D. W., DeFries, J. C., & Plomin, R. (1990). Home environment and cognitive ability of 7-year-old children in the Colorado Adoption Project: Genetic and environmental etiologies. *Developmental Psychology, 26*, 459-468.

Copranzano, R., & James, K. (1990). Some methodological considerations for the behavioral genetic analysis of work attitudes. *Journal of Applied Psychology, 75*, 433-439.

Corley, R., & Coon, H. (1991). Resemblance for TV viewing and other interest at age 7 in adoptive and nonadoptive siblings [abstract]. *Behavior Genetics, 21*, 567.

Crockenberg, S. (1986). Are temperamental differences in babies associated with predictable differences in caregivers? In J. Lerner & R. Lerner (Eds.), *Temperament and social interaction in children* (pp. 53-73). San Francisco: Jossey-Bass.

Crouter, A., & McHale, S. (1993). The long arm of the job: Influences of parental work on child rearing. In T. Luster & L. Okagaki (Eds.), *Parenting: An ecological perspective* (pp. 179-202). Hillsdale, NJ: Lawrence Erlbaum.

Daniels, D., & Plomin, R. (1985). Differential experience of siblings in the same family. *Developmental Psychology, 21*, 747-760.

Darlington, C. D. (1953). *The facts of life*. London: George Allen & Unwin.

Dawkins, R. (1983). *The extended phenotype: The long reach of the gene*. Oxford: Oxford University Press.

DeFries, J. C., Plomin, R., & Fulker, D. W. (in press). *Nature and nurture during middle childhood*. Cambridge, MA: Blackwell.

DeKay, W. T., & Buss, D. M. (1992). Human nature, individual differences, and the importance of context: Perspectives from evolutionary psychology. *Current Directions in Psychological Science, 1*, 184-189.

Dibble, E., & Cohen, D. J. (1974). Companion instruments for measuring children's competence and parental style. *Archives of General Psychiatry, 30*, 804-815.

Dix, T. H., & Grusec, J. (1983). Parental influence techniques: An attributional analysis. *Child Development, 54*, 645-652.

Dix, T. H., & Grusec, J. (1985). Parent attribution processes in the socialization of children. In I. E. Sigel (Ed.), *Parental belief systems* (pp. 201-233). Hillsdale, NJ: Lawrence Erlbaum.

Dobzhansky, Th., & Penrose, L. S. (1955). Review of *The Facts of Life* by C. D. Darlington. *Annals of Human Genetics, 19*, 75-77.

Dornbush, S., Ritter, P., Leiderman, P., Roberts, D., & Fraleigh, M. (1987). The relation of parenting style to adolescent school performance. *Child Development, 58*, 1244-1257.

Dunn, J., & Plomin, R. (1986). Determinants of maternal behavior toward three-year-old siblings. *British Journal of Developmental Psychology, 4*, 127, 137.

Dunn, J., Plomin, R., & Daniels, D. (1986). Consistency and change in mothers' behavior toward young siblings. *Child Development, 57*, 348-356.

Dunn, J., Plomin, R., & Nettles, M. (1985). Consistency of mothers' behavior towards infant siblings. *Developmental Psychology, 21*, 1188-1195.

Dunn, J. F., Stocker, C., & Plomin, R. (1990). Assessing the relationship between young siblings. *Journal of Child Psychology and Psychiatry, 31*, 983-991.

Eaves, L., Eysenck, H. J., & Martin, N. G. (1989). *Genes, culture and personality*. New York: Academic Press.

Eaves, L. J., Hewitt, J. K., & Heath, A. C. (1988). The quantitative genetic study of human developmental change. In B. S. Weir, E. J. Eisen, M. M. Goodman, & G. Namkoong (Eds.), *Proceedings of the Second International Conference on Quantitative Genetics* (pp. 297-311). Sunderland, MA: Sinauer.

Edelman, G. M. (1992). *Bright air, brilliant fire: On the matter of the mind*. New York: Basic Books.

Edelman, G. M. (1970). The structure and function of antibodies. In F. M. Burnet (Ed.), *Immunology* (pp. 39-48). San Francisco: Freeman.

Falconer, D. S. (1981). *Introduction to quantitative genetics*. New York: Longman.

Folling, A., Mohr., O. L., & Ruud, L. (1945). *Oligophrenia phenylpyrouvica*, a recessive syndrome in man. *Norske Videnskaps/Akademi i Oslo, Matematisk-Naturvidenskapelig Klasse, 13*, 1-44.

Freeman, F. N., Holzinger, K. J., & Mitchell, B. (1928). The influence of environment on the intelligence, school achievement, and conduct of foster children. *Twenty-Seventh Yearbook of the National Society for the Study of Education, 27*, 103-217.

French, D. L., Laskov, R., & Scharff, M. D. (1989). The role of hypermutation in the generation of antibody diversity. *Science, 244*, 1152-1157.

Fulker, D. W., Baker, L. A., & Bock, R. D. (1983). Estimating components of covariance using LISREL. *Data Analyst: Communications in Computer Data Analysis, 1*, 5-8.

Fulker, D. W., & Eysenck, H. J. (1979). Nature and nurture: Heredity. In H. J. Eysenck (Ed.), *The structure and measurement of intelligence* (pp. 102-174). New York: Springer.

Galton, F. (1875). The history of twins as a criterion of the relative powers of nature and nurture. *Journal of the Anthropological Institute, 6*, 391-406.

Galton, F. (1883). *Inquiries into human faculty and its development*. London: Macmillan.

Gazzaniga, M. S. (1992). *Nature's mind: The biological roots of thinking, emotions, sexuality, language, and intelligence*. New York: Basic Books.

Gluzman, Y., & Shenk, T. (1984). *Enhancers and eukaryotic gene expression*. Cold Spring Harbor, NY: Cold Spring Harbor Laboratory.

Goldsmith, H. H. (1993). Nature-nurture issues in behavior-genetic context: Overcoming barriers to communication. In R. Plomin & G. E. McClearn (Eds.), *Nature, nurture, and psychology* (pp. 325-339). Washington, DC: APA Books.

Goodman, R., & Stevenson, J. (1991). Parental criticism and warmth toward unrecognized monozygotic twins. *Behavior and Brain Sciences, 14*, 394-395.

Goodnow, J. J., & Collins, W. A. (1990). *Development according to parents: The nature, sources, and consequences of parents' ideas*. Hillsdale, NJ: Lawrence Erlbaum.

Gottfried, A. E., & Gottfried, A. W. (1984). Home environment and mental development in middle-class children in the first three years. In A. W. Gottfried (Ed.), *Environment and early cognitive development: Longitudinal research* (pp. 57-115). New York: Academic Press.

Grunstein, M. (1992). Histones as regulators of genes. *Scientific American, 267*, 68-74.

Halverson, C. F., Jr. (1988). Remembering your parents: Reflections on the retrospective method. *Journal of Personality, 56*, 435-443.

Hanson, R. (1975). Consistency and stability of home environmental measures related to IQ. *Child Development, 46*, 470-480.

Hardy-Brown, K., & Plomin, R. (1985). Infant communicative development: Evidence from adoptive and biological families for genetic and environmental influences on rate differences. *Developmental Psychology, 21*, 378-385.

Harper, L. V. (1992). *The nurture of human behavior*. Norwood, NJ: Ablex.

Hartup, W. W. (1983). Peer relations. In E. M. Hetherington (Ed.), *Handbook of child psychology: Vol. 4. Socialization, personality, and social development* (pp. 103-196). New York: John Wiley.

Hayes, K. (1962). Genes, drives, and intellect. *Psychological Reports, 10*, 299-342.

Henderson, D., Duncan-Jones, P., Byrne, D. G., & Scott, R. (1980). Measuring social relationships: The Interview Schedule for Social Interaction. *Psychological Medicine, 10*, 723-734.

Hershberger, S. L., Lichtenstein, P., Knox, S. S., & McClearn, G. E. (in press). Genetic and environmental influences on perceptions of organizational climate. *Journal of Applied Psychology*.

Hoffman, L. W. (1991). The influence of the family environment on personality: Accounting for sibling differences. *Psychological Bulletin, 110*, 187-203.

Holahan, C. K., & Holahan, C. J. (1987). Life stress, hassles, and self-efficacy in aging: A replication and extension. *Journal of Applied Social Psychology, 17*, 574-592.

Holmes, T. H. (1979). Development and application of a quantitative measure of life change magnitude. In J. E. Barrett (Ed.), *Stress and mental disorder* (pp. 37-53). New York: Raven.

Holmes, T. H., & Rahe, R. H. (1967). The Social Readjustment Rating Scale. *Journal of Psychosomatic Research, 11*, 213-218.

Horowitz, F. D. (1993). Bridging the gap between nature and nurture: A conceptually flawed issue and the need for a comprehensive new environmentalism. In R. Plomin & G. E. McClearn (Eds.), *Nature, nurture, and psychology* (pp. 341-353). Washington, DC: APA Books.

Howes, C. (1990). Can the age of entry into child care and the quality of child care predict adjustment in kindergarten? *Developmental Psychology, 26*, 292-303.

Hunt, J. McV. (1965). Intrinsic motivation and its role in psychological development. In D. Levine (Ed.), *Nebraska Symposium on Motivation* (pp. 189-287). Lincoln: University of Nebraska Press.

Jacob, F., & Monod, J. (1961). On the regulation of gene activity. *Cold Spring Harbor Symposia on Quantitative Biology, 26*, 193-209.

Jang, K. L. (1993). *A behavioral genetic analysis of personality, personality disorder, the environment, and the search for sources of nonshared environmental influences*. Unpublished doctoral dissertation, The University of Western Ontario, London, Ontario.

Jensen, A. R. (1980). *Bias in mental testing*. New York: Free Press.

Jerne, N. (1967). Antibodies and learning: Selection versus instruction. In G. Quarton, T. Melnechuck, & F. O. Schmitt (Eds.), *The neurosciences: A study program* (Vol. 1, pp. 200-205). New York: Rockefeller University Press.

Johnson, J. H. (1986). *Life events as stressors in childhood and adolescence*. Beverly Hills, CA: Sage.

Kagan, J., Arcus, D., & Snidman, N. (1993). Nature-nurture: Where do we go from here? The idea of temperament. In R. Plomin & G. E. McClearn (Eds.), *Nature, nurture and psychology* (pp. 197-210). Washington, DC: American Psychological Association.

Kendler, K. S., Neale, M., Kessler, R., Heath, A., & Eaves, L. (in press). A twin study of recent life events and difficulties. *Archives of General Psychology.*

Kessler, R. C., Kendler, K. S., Heath, A., Neale, M. C., & Eaves, L. J. (1992). Social support, depressed mood, and adjustment to stress: A genetic epidemiologic investigation. *Journal of Personality and Social Psychology, 62,* 257-272.

Kluckholm, C., Murray, H. A., & Schneider, D. M. (Eds.). (1953). *Personality in nature, society and culture* (2nd ed.). New York: Knopf.

Kohn, M., & Schooler, C. (1983). *Work and personality: An inquiry into the impact of social stratification.* Norwood, NJ: Ablex.

Lawrence, P. A. (1992). *The making of a fly: The genetics of animal design.* Oxford: Blackwell Scientific Publications.

Lazarus, R. S., & Folkman, S. (1985). *Stress, appraisal, and coping.* New York: Springer.

Leahy, A. M. (1935). Nature-nurture and intelligence. *Genetic Psychology Monographs, 17,* 236-308.

Leder, P. (1982). The generation of antibody diversity. *Scientific American, 246,* 102-110.

Lehtovaara, A. (1938). *Psychologische Zwillingsuntersuchungen.* Helsinki: Finnish Academy of Science.

Lewin, R. (1984). Why is development so illogical? *Science, 224,* 1327-1329.

Lichtenstein, P., Harris, J. R., Pedersen, N. L., & McClearn, G. E. (in press). Socioeconomic status and physical health, how are they related? An empirical study based on twins reared apart and twins reared together. *Social Science and Medicine.*

Lichtenstein, P., & Pedersen, N. L. (1991). Genetic analyses of socioeconomic status in twins reared apart and twins reared together [abstract]. *Behavior Genetics, 21,* 728.

Lichtenstein, P., Pedersen, N. L., & McClearn, G. E. (1992). Genetic and environmental predictors of socioeconomic status [abstract]. *Behavior Genetics, 22,* 731-732.

Loehlin, J. C. (1992a). *Genes and environment in personality development.* Newbury Park, CA: Sage Publications.

Loehlin, J. C. (1992b). *Latent variable models: An introduction to factor, path, and structural analysis* (2nd ed.). Hillsdale, NJ: Lawrence Erlbaum.

Loehlin, J. C., & DeFries, J. C. (1987). Genotype-environment correlation revisited. *Behavior Genetics, 17,* 263-278.

Loehlin, J. C., Horn, J. M., & Willerman, L. (1989). Modeling IQ change: Evidence from the Texas Adoption Project. *Child Development, 60,* 993-1004.

Loehlin, J. C., & Nichols, R. C. (1976). *Heredity, environment and personality.* Austin: University of Texas Press.

Luster, T., & Dubow, E. (1991, April). *Home environment and maternal intelligence as predictors of verbal intelligence.* Paper presented to the Society for Research in Child Development, Seattle.

Lyle, J., & Hoffman, H. R. (1972). Children's use of television and other media. In E. A. Rubinstein, G. A. Comstock, & J. P. Murray (Eds.), *Television in day-to-day life: Patterns of use.* Washington, DC: Government Printing Office.

Lytton, H. (1977). Do parents create or respond to differences in twins? *Developmental Psychology, 13,* 456-459.

Lytton, H. (1980). *Parent-child interaction: The socialization process observed in twin and singleton families.* New York: Plenum.

Lytton, H. (1991). Different parental practices—Different sources of influence. *Behavioral and Brain Sciences, 14,* 399-400.

Lytton, H., Watts, D., & Dunn, B. E. (1986). Stability and predictability of cognitive and social characteristics from age 2 to age 9. *Genetic, Social and General Psychology Monographs, 112,* 361-398.

Lytton, H., Watts, D., & Dunn, B. E. (1988). Stability of genetic determination from age 2 to age 9: A longitudinal twin study. *Social Biology, 35,* 62-73.

Maccoby, E., & Martin, J. A. (1983). Socialization in the context of the family: Parent-child interaction. In P. H. Mussen (Ed.), *Handbook of child psychology: Vol. 4. Socialization, personality, and social development* (4th ed.) (pp. 1-101). New York: John Wiley.

Mack, K. J., & Mack, P. A. (1992). Introduction of transcription factors in somatosensory cortex after tactile stimulation. *Molecular Brain Research, 12,* 141-149.

Maclean, N. (1989). *Genes and gene regulation.* London: Edward Arnold.

Mancuso, J. C., & Lehrer, R. (1986). Cognitive processes during reactions to rule violation. In R. D. Ashmore & D. M. Brodzinsky (Eds.), *Thinking about the family: Views of parent and children* (pp. 67-93). Hillsdale, NJ: Lawrence Erlbaum.

Manke, B., McGuire, S., Reiss, D., Hetherington, E. M., & Plomin, R. (1993). *Genetic contributions to children's extrafamilial social interactions: Teachers, friends, and peers.* Manuscript in preparation.

Martin, N. G., & Eaves, L. J. (1977). The genetical analysis of covariance structure. *Heredity, 38,* 79-95.

Matheny, A. P., Jr. (1980). Bayley's Infant Behavior Record: Behavioral components and twin analyses. *Child Development, 54,* 356-360.

Matheny, A. P., Jr. (1988). Accidental injuries. In D. K. Routh (Ed.), *Handbook of pediatric psychology* (pp. 108-134). New York: Guilford Press.

Mayr, E. (1982). *The growth of biological thought.* Cambridge, MA: Harvard University Press.

McCall, R. B. (1977). Challenges to a science of developmental psychology. *Child Development, 48,* 333-344.

McCall, R. B. (1981). Nature-nurture and the two realms of development: A proposed integration with respect to mental development. *Child Development, 52,* 1-12.

McCrae, R. R., & Costa, P. T., Jr. (1988). Recalled parent-child relations and adult personality. *Journal of Personality, 56,* 417-432.

McGue, M., Bouchard, T. J., Lykken, D. T., & Finkel, D. (1991). On genes, environment, and experience. *Behavioral and Brain Sciences, 14,* 400-401.

McGue, M., & Lykken, D. T. (1992). Genetic influence on risk of divorce. *Psychological Science, 3,* 368-373.

McGuffin, P., & Katz, R. (1993). Genes, adversity and depression. In R. Plomin & G. E. McClearn (Eds.), *Nature, nurture, and psychology* (pp. 217-230). Washington, DC: American Psychological Association.

McGuffin, P., Katz, R., & Bebbington, P. (1988). The Camberwell Collaborative Depression Study. III. Depression and adversity in the relatives of depressed probands. *British Journal of Psychiatry, 152,* 775-782.

McGuire, S., Reiss, D., Hetherington, E. M., & Plomin, R. (1992). Genetic mediation of environment-outcome associations during adolescence: A study of twins, full siblings, and step siblings [abstract]. *Behavior Genetics, 22,* 736.

McGurk, H. (1992). A comment on child effects in socialization research: Some conceptual and data analysis issues. *Social Development, 1,* 244-246.

McKenchie, G. E. (1974). *Environmental response inventory.* Palo Alto, CA: Consulting Psychologists Press.

Mello, C. V., Vicario, D. S., & Clayton, D. F. (1992). Song presentation induces gene expression in the songbird forebrain. *Proceedings of the National Academic of Sciences USA, 89,* 6818-6820.

Mendel, G. (1866). Versuche Über Pflanzenhybriden. [Experiments in plant hybridization.] *Verhandlungen des Naturs-forschunden Vereines in Bruenn, 4,* 3-47.

Moos, R. (1981). *Work Environment Scale manual.* Palo Alto, CA: Consulting Psychologist Press.

Moster, M. (1990). *Stressful life events: Genetic and environmental components and their relationship to affective symptomatology.* Unpublished doctoral dissertation, University of Minnesota, Minneapolis.

Neale, M. C., & Cardon, L. R. (1992). *Methodology for genetic studies of twins and families.* Dordrecht: Kluwer Academic Publishers.

Neiderhiser, J. M. (in press). Family environment in early childhood, outcomes in middle childhood, and genetic mediation. In J. C. DeFries, R. Plomin, & D. W. Fulker (Eds.), *Nature and nurture during middle childhood.* Cambridge, MA: Blackwell.

Neiderhiser, J. M., Plomin, R., Lichtenstein, P., Pedersen, N. L., & McClearn, G. E. (1992). The influence of life events on depressive symptoms over time [abstract]. *Behavior Genetics, 22,* 740.

O'Connor, T., Hetherington, E. M., Reiss, D., & Plomin, R. (in press). A twin-sibling study of parent-adolescent interaction. *Child Development.*

Paykel, E. S. (1983). Methodological aspects of life events research. *Journal of Psychosomatic Research, 27,* 341-352.

Pearl, D., Bouthilet, L., & Lazar, J. (Eds.). (1982). *Television and behavior: Ten years of scientific progress and implications for the eighties* (Vol. 1). Washington, DC: Government Printing Office.

Pedersen, N. L., McClearn, G. E., Plomin, R., & Nesselroade, J. R. (1992). Effects of early rearing environment on twin similarity in the last half of the life span. *British Journal of Developmental Psychology, 10,* 255-267.

Pedersen, N. L., McClearn, G. E., Plomin, R., Nesselroade, J. R., Berg, S., & DeFaire, U. (1991). The Swedish Adoption/Twin Study of Aging: An update. *Acta Geneticae Medicae et Gemellologiae, 40,* 7-20.

Pedersen, N. L., Plomin, R., McClearn, G. E., & Friberg, L. (1988). Neuroticism, extraversion, and related traits in adult twins reared apart and reared together. *Journal of Personality and Social Psychology, 55,* 950-957.

Persson, G. (1980). Prevalence of mental disorders in a 70-year-old urban population. *Acta Psychiatrica Scandinavica, 62*, 112-118.

Perusse, D., Neale, M. C., Heath, A. C., & Eaves, L. J. (1992). Human parental behavior: Evidence for genetic influence and implications for gene-culture transmission [abstract]. *Behavior Genetics, 22*, 744-745.

Phillips, K., & Matheny, A. P., Jr. (1993). *Quantitative genetic analysis of injury liability in infants and toddlers.* Manuscript submitted for publication.

Pike, A., Manke, B., Hetherington, E. M., Reiss, D., & Plomin, R. (1993). *Differential experiences of adolescent siblings: Genetic and environmental influences.* Manuscript in preparation.

Plomin, R. (1986). *Development, genetics, and psychology.* Hillsdale, NJ: Lawrence Erlbaum.

Plomin, R. (1990a). *Nature and nurture: An introduction to human behavioral genetics.* Pacific Grove, CA: Brooks/Cole.

Plomin, R. (1990b). The role of inheritance in behavior. *Science, 248*, 183-188.

Plomin, R. (1993). Nature and nurture: Perspective and prospective. In R. Plomin & G. E. McClearn (Eds.), *Nature, nurture, and psychology* (pp. 457-493). Washington, DC: American Psychological Association.

Plomin, R., & Bergeman, C. S. (1991a). The nature of nurture: Genetic influence on "environmental" measures. *Behavior and Brain Sciences, 14*, 373-427. (With Open Peer Commentary)

Plomin, R., & Bergeman, C. S. (1991b). The nature of nurture: Genetic influence on "environmental" measures. *Behavior and Brain Sciences, 14*, 414-424. (Response to commentaries)

Plomin, R., Corley, R., DeFries, J. C., & Fulker, D. W. (1990). Individual differences in television viewing in early childhood: Nature as well as nurture. *Psychological Science, 1*, 371-377.

Plomin, R., & Daniels, D. (1987). Why are children in the same family so different from each other? *The Behavioral and Brain Sciences, 10*, 1-16.

Plomin, R., & DeFries, J. C. (1979). Multivariate behavioral genetic analysis of twin data on scholastic abilities. *Behavior Genetics, 9*, 505-517.

Plomin, R., & DeFries, J. C. (1981). Multivariate behavioral genetics and development: Twin studies. In L. Gedda, P. Parisi, & W. E. Nance (Eds.), *Progress in clinical and biological research. Twin research 3: Part B. Intelligence, personality, and development* (Vol. 69B, pp. 25-33). New York: Alan F. Liss.

Plomin, R., & DeFries, J. C. (1985). *Origins of individual differences in infancy: The Colorado Adoption Project.* New York: Academic Press.

Plomin, R., DeFries, J. C., & Fulker, D. F. (1988). *Nature and nurture during infancy and early childhood.* New York: Cambridge University Press.

Plomin, R., DeFries, J. C., & Loehlin, J. C. (1977). Genotype-environment interaction and correlation in the analysis of human behavior. *Psychological Bulletin, 84*, 309-322.

Plomin, R., DeFries, J. C., & McClearn, G. E. (1990). *Behavioral genetics: A primer* (2nd ed.). New York: Freeman.

Plomin, R., & Hershberger, S. (1991). Genotype-environment interaction. In T. D. Wachs & R. Plomin (Eds.), *Conceptualization and measurement of organism-environment interaction* (pp. 29-43). Washington, DC: American Psychological Association.

Plomin, R., Lichtenstein, P., Pedersen, N. L., McClearn, G. E., & Nesselroade, J. R. (1990). Genetic influence on life events during the last half of the life span. *Psychology and Aging, 5,* 25-30.

Plomin, R., Loehlin, J. C., & DeFries, J. C. (1985). Genetic and environmental components of "environmental" influences. *Developmental Psychology, 21,* 391-402.

Plomin, R., McClearn, G. E., Pedersen, N. L., Nesselroade, J. R., & Bergeman, C. S. (1988). Genetic influence on childhood family environment perceived retrospectively from the last half of the life span. *Developmental Psychology, 24,* 738-745.

Plomin, R., McClearn, G. E., Pedersen, N. L., Nesselroade, J. R., & Bergeman, C. S., (1989). Genetic influence on adults' ratings of their current family environment. *Journal of Marriage and the Family, 51,* 791-803.

Plomin, R., & Neiderhiser, J. M. (1992a). Genetics and experience. *Current Directions in Psychological Science, 1,* 160-163.

Plomin, R., & Neiderhiser, J. M. (1992b). Quantitative genetics, molecular genetics, and intelligence. *Intelligence, 15,* 369-387.

Plomin, R., Reiss, D., Hetherington, E. M., & Howe, G. (in press). Nature and nurture: Genetic influence on measures of the family environment. *Developmental Psychology.*

Plomin, R., Scheier, M. F., Bergeman, C. S., Pedersen, N. L., Nesselroade, J. R., & McClearn, G. E. (1992). Optimism, pessimism, and mental health: A twin/adoption analysis. *Personality and Individual Differences, 13,* 921-930.

Reiss, D., Plomin, R., Hetherington, E. M., Howe, G., Rovine, M., Tryon, A., & Stanley, M. (1994). The separate worlds of teenage siblings: An introduction to the study of the nonshared environment and adolescent development. In E. M. Hetherington, D. Reiss, & R. Plomin (Eds.), *Separate social worlds of siblings: Impact of nonshared environment on development* (pp. 63-109). Hillsdale, NJ: Lawrence Erlbaum.

Rende, R. D. (in press). The stress of first grade and its relation to behavior problems in school. In J. C. DeFries, R. Plomin, & D. W. Fulker (Eds.), *Nature and nurture in middle childhood.* Cambridge, MA: Blackwell.

Rende, R. D., & Plomin, R. (1991). Child and parent perceptions of the upsettingness of major life events. *Journal of Child Psychology and Psychiatry, 32,* 627-633.

Rende, R. D., & Plomin, R. (1992). Diathesis-stress models of psychopathology: A quantitative genetic perspective. *Applied and Preventive Psychology, 1,* 177-182.

Rende, R. D., Slomkowski, C. L., Stocker, C., Fulker, D. W., & Plomin, R. (1992). Genetic and environmental influences on maternal and sibling interaction in middle childhood: A sibling adoption study. *Developmental Psychology, 28,* 484-490.

Renninger, K. A., Hidi, S., & Krapp, A. (1992). *The role of interest in learning and development.* Hillsdale, NJ: Lawrence Erlbaum.

Rice, T., Fulker, D. W., DeFries, J. C., & Plomin, R. (1988). Path analysis of IQ during infancy and early childhood and an index of home environment in the Colorado Adoption Project. *Intelligence, 12,* 27-45.

Roff, M., Sells, S. B., & Golden, M. M. (1972). *Social adjustment and personality development in children.* Minneapolis: University of Minnesota Press.

Rose, S. (1992). Selective attention. *Nature, 360,* 426-427.

Ross, L., & Nisbett, R. E. (1991). *The person and the situation*. New York: McGraw-Hill.

Rowe, D. C. (1981). Environmental and genetic influences on dimensions of perceived parenting: A twin study. *Developmental Psychology, 17*, 203-208.

Rowe, D. C. (1983). A biometrical analysis of perceptions of family environment: A study of twin and singleton sibling kinships. *Child Development, 54*, 416-423.

Rowe, D. C. (1989). Families and peers: Another look at the nature-nurture question. In T. J. Berndt & G. W. Ladd (Eds.), *Peer relationships in child development* (pp. 174-299). New York: John Wiley.

Rowe, D. C., Callor, S., Harmon-Losoya, S. G., & Goldsmith, H. H. (1992). The transmission of parenting behavior: Rearing or genetics? [abstract]. *Behavior Genetics, 22*, 750-751.

Rowe, D. C., & Waldman, I. D. (1993). The question "how" reconsidered. In R. Plomin & G. E. McClearn (Eds.), *Nature, nurture, and psychology* (pp. 353-373). Washington, DC: American Psychological Association.

Rowe, J. W., & Kahn, R. L. (1987). Human aging: Usual and successful. *Science, 237*, 143-149.

Rubin, Z., & Sloman, J. (1984). How parents influence their children's friendships. In M. Lewis (Ed.), *Beyond the dyad* (pp. 223-250). New York: Plenum.

Russell, A., & Russell, G. (1992). Child effects in socialization research: Some conceptual and data analysis issues. *Social Development, 1*, 163-184.

Rutter, M. (1989). Pathways from childhood to adult life. *Journal of Child Psychology and Psychiatry, 30*, 23-51.

Rutter, M., & Pickles, A. (1991). Person-environment interactions: Concepts, mechanisms, and implication for data analysis. In T. D. Wachs & R. Plomin (Eds.), *Conceptualization and measurement of organism-environment interaction* (pp. 105-141). Washington, DC: American Psychological Association.

Rutter, M., Silberg, J., & Simonoff, E. (1993). Whither behavior genetics? A developmental psychopathology perspective. In R. Plomin & G. E. McClearn (Eds.), *Nature, nurture, and psychology* (pp. 355-373). Washington, DC: American Psychological Association.

Sameroff, A., & Chandler, M. (1975). Reproductive risk and the continuum of care taking causality. In F. Horowitz (Ed.), *Review of child development research 4* (pp. 187-244). New York: John Wiley.

Sarason, I. G., Johnson, J. H., & Siegel, J. H. (1978). Assessing the impact of life changes: Development of the Life Experiences Survey. *Journal of Consulting and Clinical Psychology, 46*, 932-946.

Saudino, K. J. (1993). *A sibling adoption analysis of items of the Home Observation for Measurement of the Environment*. Manuscript in preparation.

Scarr, S. (1968). Environmental bias in twin studies. *Eugenics Quarterly, 15*, 34-40.

Scarr, S. (1992). Developmental theories for the 1990s: Development and individual differences. *Child Development, 63*, 1-19.

Scarr, S., & Carter-Saltzman, L. (1979). Twin method: Defense of a critical assumption. *Behavior Genetics, 9*, 527-542.

Scarr, S., & McCartney, K. (1983). How people make their own environments: A theory of genotype-environment effects. *Child Development, 54*, 424-435.

Schaefer, E. S. (1965). Children's reports of parental behavior: An inventory. *Child Development, 36*, 413-424.

Seligman, M. E. P. (1991). *Learned optimism*. New York: Knopf.

Selye, H. (1936). A syndrome produced by diverse nocuous agents. *Nature, 138,* 32.

Shweder, R. A. (1990). Cultural psychology—what is it? In J. W. Stigler, R. A. Shweder, & G. Herdt (Eds.), *Cultural psychology* (pp. 1-43). New York: Cambridge University Press.

Skodak, M., & Skeels, H. M. (1949). A final follow-up of one hundred adopted children. *Journal of Genetic Psychology, 75,* 85-125.

Slabach, E., Morrow, J., & Wachs, T. D. (1991). Questionnaire measurement of infant and child temperament: Current status and future directions. In J. Strelau & A. Angleitner (Eds.), *Explorations in temperament* (pp. 205-234). New York: Plenum.

Smith, R. T. (1965). A comparison of socio-environmental factors in monozygotic and dizygotic twins, testing an assumption. In S. G. Vandenberg (Ed.), *Methods and goals in human behavior genetics* (pp. 45-62). New York: Academic Press.

Tambs, K., Sundet, J. M., Magnus, P., & Berg, K. (1989). Genetic and environmental contributions to the covariance between occupational status, educational attainment and IQ: A study of twins. *Behavior Genetics, 19,* 209-222.

Taubman, P. (1976). The determinants of earnings: Genetics, family and other environments: A study of white male twins. *American Economic Review, 66,* 858-870.

Taylor, S. E. (1989). *Positive illusions*. New York: Basic Books.

Teasdale, T. W. (1979). Social class correlations among adoptees and their biological and adoptive parents. *Behavior Genetics, 9,* 103-114.

Teasdale, T. W., & Owen, D. R. (1981). Social class correlations among separately adopted siblings and unrelated individuals adopted together. *Behavioral Genetics, 11,* 577-688.

Thoits, P. A. (1983). Dimensions of life events that influence psychological distress: An evaluation and syntheses of the literature. In H. A. Kaplan (Ed.), *Psychological stress: Trends in theory and research* (pp. 33-103). New York: Academic Press.

Thoits, P. A. (1986). Social support as coping assistance. *Journal of Consulting and Clinical Psychology, 54,* 416-423.

Thompson, L. A., Fulker, D. W., DeFries, J. C., & Plomin, R. (1986). Multivariate genetic analysis of "environmental" influences on infant cognitive development. *British Journal of Developmental Psychology, 4,* 347-353.

Trickett, E. J., & Moss, R. H. (1976). *Classroom Environment Scale manual*. Palo Alto, CA: Consulting Psychologists Press.

Tsuang, M. T., Lyons, M. J., Eisen, S. A., True, W. T., Goldberg, J., & Henderson, W. (1992). A twin study of drug exposure and initiation of use [abstract]. *Behavior Genetics, 22,* 756.

Turkheimer, E., Lovett, G., Robinette, C. D., & Gottesman, I. I. (1992). The heritability of divorce: New data and theoretical implications [abstract]. *Behavior Genetics, 22,* 757.

Wachs, T. D. (1986). Models of physical environment action. In A. Gottfried (Ed.), *Play interactions: The contribution of play material and parent involvement to child development* (pp. 253-278). Lexington, MA: Lexington.

Wachs, T. D. (1991). Environmental considerations in studies of organism-environment interaction with nonextreme groups. In T. D. Wachs & R. Plomin (Eds.),

*Conceptualization and measurement of organism-environment interaction* (pp. 44-67). Washington, DC: American Psychological Association.

Wachs, T. D. (1992). *The nature of nurture.* Newbury Park, CA: Sage Publications.

Wachs, T. D. (1993). The nature-nurture gap: What we have here is a failure to collaborate. In R. Plomin & G. E. McClearn (Eds.), *Nature, nurture, and psychology* (pp. 375-391). Washington, DC: American Psychological Association.

Wachs, T. D., & Gruen, G. (1982). *Early experience and human development.* New York: Plenum.

Wachs, T. D., & Plomin, R. (Eds.). (1991). *Conceptualization and measurement of organism-environment interaction.* Washington, DC: American Psychological Association.

Wahlsten, D. (1990). Insensitivity of the analysis of variance to heredity-environment interaction. *Behavioral and Brain Sciences, 13,* 109-161.

Waldman, I. D., & Weinberg, R. A. (1991). The need for collaboration between behavior geneticists and environmentally oriented investigators in developmental research. *Behavioral and Brain Sciences, 14,* 412-413.

Watson, J. B. (1925). *Behaviorism.* New York: Norton.

Watson, J. B. (1928). *Psychological care of infant and child.* New York: Norton.

Watson, J. D., & Crick, F. H. C. (1953). Molecular structure of nucleic acids. A structure for deoxyribose nucleic acids. *Nature, 171,* 737-738.

West, P. (1991). Rethinking the health selection explanation for health inequalities. *Social Science and Medicine, 32,* 373-384.

White, R. W. (1959). Motivation reconsidered: The concept of competence. *Psychological Review, 66,* 297-333.

Wierzbicki, M. (1989). Twin's responses to pleasant, unpleasant, and life events. *Journal of genetic psychology, 150,* 135-145.

Wilson, E. O. (1975). *Sociobiology, the new synthesis.* Cambridge, MA: Harvard University Press.

Wilson, P. T. (1934). A study of twins with special reference to heredity as a factor determining differences in environment. *Human Biology, 6,* 324-354.

Wohlwill, J. F. (1973). *The study of behavioral development.* New York: Academic Press.

Yeates, K. O., MacPhee, D., Campbell, F. A., & Ramey, C. T. (1983). Maternal IQ and home environment as determinants of early childhood intellectual competence: A developmental analysis. *Developmental Psychology, 19,* 731-739.

Yoshinaga, S. K., Peterson, C. L., Herskowitz, I., & Yamamoto, K. R. (1992). Roles of SWI1, SWI2, and SWI3 proteins for transcriptional enhancement by steroid receptors. *Science, 258,* 1598-1604.

Zazzo, R. (1960). *Les jumeaux, le couple et la personne* [Twins, the pair, and the person]. Paris: Presses Universitaires de France.

# Index

# About the Author

Robert Plomin is Distinguished Professor and Director of the Center for Developmental and Health Genetics, College of Health and Human Development, The Pennsylvania State University. After receiving his Ph.D. in Psychology from The University of Texas, Austin, in 1974, he moved to the University of Colorado at Boulder and, in 1986, to The Pennsylvania State University. His research has focused on the application of genetic research strategies to the investigation of behavioral development. He has published more than 200 papers in the field of behavioral genetics and has written 10 books—most recently, *Development, Genetics, and Psychology*, (1986); *Nature and Nurture in Infancy and Early Childhood* (with J. C. DeFries and D. W. Fulker, 1988); *Separate Lives: Why Siblings Are So Different* (with J. Dunn, 1990); *Behavioral Genetics* (with J. C. DeFries and G. E. McClearn, 1990); and *Nature and Nurture: An Introduction to Human Behavioral Genetics* (1990)—in addition to five edited books. He is a past president of the International Behavior Genetics Association. During 1993, he was an American Psychological Association Distinguished Scientist Lecturer, a James McKeen Cattell Fellow, a Fulbright Scholar, and a Fogarty Senior International Fellow.